# CEYLON

## PAST AND PRESENT

REFLECTIONS
The Rock of Sigiriya.

Frontispiece

# CEYLON
# PAST AND PRESENT

C. M. ENRIQUEZ

*WITH MAPS AND ILLUSTRATIONS*

GYAN

*Published by*

Gyan Publishing House
5, Ansari Road
Daryaganj, New Delhi-110002
Phone: 011-47034999, 9811692060
E-mail: books@gyanbooks.com

*Distribution Network*
gyanbooks.com
India, USA, Canada, UK, Australia, France



ISBN : 9788121232210 (PB)
First Published, London

2nd Impression 2020

*Printed at:* Gyan Press, Delhi.



**Ceylon Past and Present**
Author: C. M. Enriquez

# CEYLON PAST AND PRESENT

By

**Major C. M. ENRIQUEZ, F.R.G.S.**

2/20 Burma Rifles

("*THEOPHILUS*")

"*Ibi Cinnamomi Odorantis*"

WITH MAPS AND ILLUSTRATIONS

*Publishers since 1812*

**HURST & BLACKETT, LTD.**
**PATERNOSTER HOUSE, E.C. 4**

TO

MY COUSINS

HONOR AND GLADYS

AND TO MY AUNT

MRS. E. T. BRIGHT

THIS BOOK IS AFFECTIONATELY DEDICATED

IN RECOGNITION OF MANY KINDNESSES

Here, surely Eve, outcast and wandering far,
Dried her slow tears and ran from tree to tree
Calling to God in ecstasy
To see this bud that glitters like a star
Or breathe the fragrance of this stream-fed flower,
And after, in the night's first hour,
Stood hand in hand
With Adam in this Eden-haunted land
To hear, soft-breathing like a child asleep,
The chiming cadence of the guardian deep.

DORIS WILSON.

# CONTENTS

## BOOK I. CEYLON—PAST



## BOOK II. CEYLON—PRESENT

CONTENTS



## APPENDICES

# LIST OF ILLUSTRATIONS

## LIST OF ILLUSTRATIONS

# INTRODUCTION

The oldest name of Ceylon, and one by which it is still known in many Oriental countries, is *Lanka.* The name of a south Indian river, the *Tamrapani,* so it is supposed, was anciently applied to it, and corrupted to *Tambapani,* the *Taprobane* of the Greeks. The word *Sinhaladivipa* (Island of the Lion Race) passed to *Selediba, Serendiva, Serendib,* and so to the Arabian *Selan Diva,*[1] the Portuguese *Ceilao,* the Dutch *Zeilan* and the English *Ceylon.*

With the exception of Egypt and Babylon, there is no country perhaps whose lost history has been more dramatically restored than that of Ceylon. A hundred years ago there existed merely a legend of Rama's battle with the Apes, a tradition of Adam's Peak, and such confused items of history as Valentyne had collected and published in Dutch in 1726. Knox, escaping in 1679 from a long captivity among the Sinhales, had brought home stories of "a world of hewn stone pillars" which he had passed during his flight through Anuradhapura.[2] His narrative was printed in 1817. Nearly a century and a half after Knox's journey,

[1] Knox's *History of Ceylon,* page 2.
[2] Knox's *History of Ceylon,* Part IV, page 334.

a pioneer officer, Lieut. Fagan, forcing his way through almost impenetrable undergrowth in 1820 had come face to face with a colossal statue gazing out at him from the foliage. Of other relics of a lost civilization, our Portuguese and Dutch predecessors seem to have had no suspicion.

Then, in 1826, a book was found by an Englishman capable of appreciating it: and it transpired that Ceylon had kept a dynastic history, second in importance only to that of China. Old generations were made to live again with an amazing wealth of detail, and with a charming humanity. Authentic history was pushed back to a period nearly four centuries B.C. Since that revelation, the works of contemporary Chinese pilgrims have corroborated the story. The spade of the excavator has uncovered monuments whose splendour we could hardly have believed from mere manuscript records. But here was ocular demonstration, when the forest was pushed back from sites which it had overwhelmed. And now the Archæologist has brought to bear that critical analysis which is separating the truth from a mass of incoherence and exaggeration. It is a wonderful feat, and one of which we British may be proud—the more so because we are so often accused of destroying what is indigenous and traditional in the East by our cold materialism. Here at least, we have restored to the Orient that which even tradition had lost: for upon the proud civilization of Ceylon remorseless Tamil raiders had 'let in the jungle': and the lowlands, which had once blossomed like a garden, were engulfed by forests that encumber it to this day. Flourishing populations had dwindled to nothing. The great lakes of a unique irrigation system had spilled their waters over the land, turning it into a malarious swamp. And gradually, as the centuries gathered and grew, Ancient Ceylon, with all its glories, faded from the memory of man.

To-day the waters have returned again to the lakes. The canals flow as of old, and in a century the population has been almost quadrupled. Ancient capitals, locked in the relentless grip of forest roots, have been released, and sleep now in placid dignity upon open lawns. The bears have been driven from the monasteries. Elephants no longer stand on the tops of pagodas that once rivalled St. Paul's in height. A dead country has been restored: and with it the people who endowed it with romance. Stout old Walagam Bahu lives again: and in the remotest age we see the kind and gracious figure of Mahinda, the Apostle of Enlightenment.

. . . . .

That is the story we have to tell in the first part of this book. We come eventually to our own times, when Ceylon, like a rich and lovely queen, gathers up the converging routes of modern trade. The traffic of the East pauses on its way at her harbour. A network of roads crosses her fair provinces. The palm tree fringes her coasts: rubber and tea pour their riches into her lap. Such is modern Ceylon, that has achieved wealth and beauty the like of which the Ancients never knew.

Let us then ring up the curtain and watch the actors move across the stage with all their little tricks and affectations. So shall we see Tissa 'Beloved of the Gods' and his great lieutenant: the kingly forms of Dutthagamini and Maha Sen: Kassiyappa the villain: Prakrama the hero. There shall be scenes of magnificence and of abasement. After Success, the Four Horsemen shall be loosed. Then come fire and sword, and a book from the West. And so the curtain falls to a merry banging of Jazz.

> "Into this Universe, and *Why* not knowing
> Nor *Whence*, like Water willy-nilly flowing:
> And out of it, as Wind along the Waste,
> I know not *Whither*, willy-nilly blowing."

# BOOK I

# CEYLON—PAST

# CEYLON PAST AND PRESENT

## CHAPTER I

### THE GEOLOGICAL HISTORY OF CEYLON

1. The island of Ceylon is 160 miles long from north to south, and about 140 miles broad. Situated as it is, in warm tropical seas, isolated from, and yet related to, the Asiatic Continent, it presents many absorbing problems akin to those of the great islands of the Malay Archipelago. Roughly speaking, it consists of an ancient mountain mass, surrounded by low plains of comparatively recent origin.

2. The most striking feature in the geology of Ceylon is the fact that the island does not appear to have been deeply submerged in the ocean at any time. As its human history is ancient, so also is its geological and zoological history. Wayland calls the central mass of Crystalline Rocks 'Archæan,' and Walt[1] has described them as belonging to the oldest geological period. From the absence of any large

[1] *Spolia Zeylanica*, Vol. X, page 1.

accumulation of sedimentary strata, it is assumed that throughout the earth's manifold oscillations, Ceylon has shared in those movements only to a limited degree.

3. Coomaraswamy[1] says with regard to the Crystalline Rocks, that it is safest to speak of them as 'Granulites,' and as belonging to the Charnockite series of Ceylon and Southern India. "If we enquire into the nature of these rocks, we are first struck by their appearance in the field suggestive of sedimentary origin. It is not surprising that the conspicuous bedded character, varied mineral composition, and local abundance of alternating beds of limestone, should have led to the supposition that such a gneissose series as we have here to deal with, represents the highly metamorphosed remains of some ancient sedimentary series. Closer examination of the rocks, however, reveals but little in support of such a view Their mineral composition is found to indicate a chemical constitution differing in important respecs from that of the great majority of sedimentary rocks, but similar to that of many well-known types of deep-seated igneous rock. Moreover, when we come to examine the foliation or mineral banding so characteristic of the Ceylon rocks, we see that there is rather a lenticular than a definitely parallel structure, and also

[1] *Spolia Zeylanica*, Vol. I, page 106.

GRANULITE

Smooth and flawless hills are characteristic of Ceylon. They are, in fact, titanic boulders.

*Facing page 4*

that some definite relation is evident between the lighter-coloured (more acid) rock-types and those of darker colour—the more basic. . . . It may be assumed with safety that at least the greater part of Ceylon rocks, so far as at present known, are of igneous origin, and that their well-banded appearance results from the drawing out (by a flowing movement) of the various parts of a heterogeneous magma, probably during its gradual consolidation under conditions of great pressure. The observed relations of the acid and basic varieties show that the latter types were amongst the earliest products of the magma, the more acid types as usual crystallizing later, and having a more or less intrusive relation towards the more basic. . . . Probably the rocks crystallized at a great depth. The absence of even ancient sedimentary rocks overlying the granulites, shows that denudation has long been at work in Ceylon. . . . It is probable that the Charnockite series is of pre-Palæozoic or Archæan Age." Sapphires and other precious stones are found near Ratanpura.

4. "At whatever period the mountains were raised," says Tennent,[1] "the centre of maximum energy must have been in the vicinity of Adam's Peak, the group immediately surrounding which has thus acquired an elevation of from six to eight thousand

[1] Tennent's *Ceylon*, Vol. I, page 14.

feet above the sea. (Adam's Peak, itself only the fourth highest mountain, is 7360 feet). The uplifting force seems to have been from south-west to north-east: and although there is much confusion in many of the ridges, the lower ones, and especially those to the south and west of Adam's Peak, manifest a remarkable tendency to run in parallel ranges. . . . Detached hills of great altitude are rare, the most celebrated being that of Mahintale, which overlooks the sacred city of Anarajapoora." But in the north of the Island outcrops of granulite, as at Sigiriya and Yapahuwa, are a common feature. Both these peaks, like similar ones in the Dekkan, have been used as rock fortresses.

5. "The crest of the Ceylon mountains is of stratified crystalline rock, especially gneiss, with intrusive veins of quartz; and through this, granite has been everywhere intruded, destroying the riven strata, and tilting them at all angles to the horizon. The great geological feature of the island is this profusion of gneiss, and the various new forms arising from its disintegration. In the mountains, with the exception of occasional beds of dolomite, no more recent formations over-lie it. From the period of its first upheaval, the gneiss has undergone no second submersion, and the soil which covers it in these lofty altitudes is formed almost entirely by its decay."

6. "In the lower ranges of the hills, gigantic portions of gneiss rise conspicuously, so detached from the original chain, and so rounded by the action of the atmosphere, that, but for their prodigious dimensions, they might be regarded as boulders. Close under one of these cylindrical masses, 600 feet in height, and upwards of three miles in length, lies one of the ancient capitals (Kornegalle) and the great temple of Dambool is constructed under the hollow edge of another."

7. The plains that occupy the surrounding lower portions of the Island are largely composed of soil formed by the disintegration of the gneiss, and carried down by the rivers of which there are several of considerable size. "But," says Tennent, "in addition to these factors, the land for ages has been slowly rising from the sea, and terraces abounding in marine shells, imbedded in agglutinated sand, occur in situations far above high-water mark. . . . These recent formations present themselves in a still more striking form in the north of the Island, the greater portion of which may be regarded as the joint production of the coral polypi, and the currents, which for the greater portion of the year set impetuously towards the south. Coming laden with alluvial matter collected along the coast of Coromandel, and

meeting with obstacles south of Point Calamere, they have deposited their burthens on the coral reefs: and these having been gradually raised above the sea-level, and covered deeply by sand drifts, have formed the peninsula of Jaffna and the plains that trend westward till they unite with the narrow causeway of Adam's Bridge, itself raised by the same agencies, and annually added to by the influence of tides and monsoons."

8. But though Ceylon is obviously an appendage of India, it is essentially related, both geologically and zoologically, to the southern part of the peninsula only. Blamford has pointed out that the great plains of the Ganges were, till quite recent times, covered by seas which separated Southern India from the Himalayas, just as now the Mediterranean divides Africa from Europe. The Gangetic plain, which severs the Indian fauna into two great sub-regions, "forms a geological boundary of the highest importance."[1] But while the *flora* and *fauna* of Ceylon are closely related to those of Southern India, they have at the same time a more remote relationship to those of Africa, Madagascar and the Malay Archipelago. These are points that indicate the existence of a great continent (now lost) which in Tertiary times stretched from Southern India and Ceylon to Madagascar on

[1] *Spolia Zeylanica*, Vol. I, page 3.

the one hand, and to Malaya on the other.[1] Of these connections, that with Madagascar was probably the most ancient.

9. Nevertheless, as Willey has pointed out,[2] "many of the characteristic forms of the Malay Peninsula are conspicuous by their absence in Ceylon, as, for instance, the flying Lemur amongst mammals, the flying lizard amongst reptiles, and the robber crab amongst crustacea." On the contrary, Malayan affinities are suggested by the presence of Bligh's Whistling Thrush, and the red-faced Malkoha, both peculiar to Ceylon, but closely related to species from Java, Sumatra, and the Malay Peninsula. Any connection with Java argues a great antiquity, because Java has been isolated from other Malayan regions since a very remote period.

10. The only Ceylon Lemur (*Loris gracilis*), and the single Sinhalese Chameleon (*Chamaeleo calcaratus*), and amongst birds the Drongo (*Dicruridae*), point to connection with Madagascar. So also do some of the snails. Those of Ceylon are highly peculiar, and the largest and commonest of them (*Acavus*), which are often found on tree-trunks and fences, are not only closely related to the Madagascar genus *Helicophanta*, but also to the Australian genus *Panda*.

[1] W. E. Wait, *Spolia Zeylanica*, Vol. X, page 5.

[2] *Spolia Zeylanica*, Vol. I, page 6.

At least two Ceylon butterflies—*Byblia violae* and *Aphnaeusa lohita lazularia*—have near relatives in South Africa.

11. Similar relationships have been observed in the marine *fauna*, and Alcock expresses the opinion that "Peninsula India and Ceylon formed, in ancient

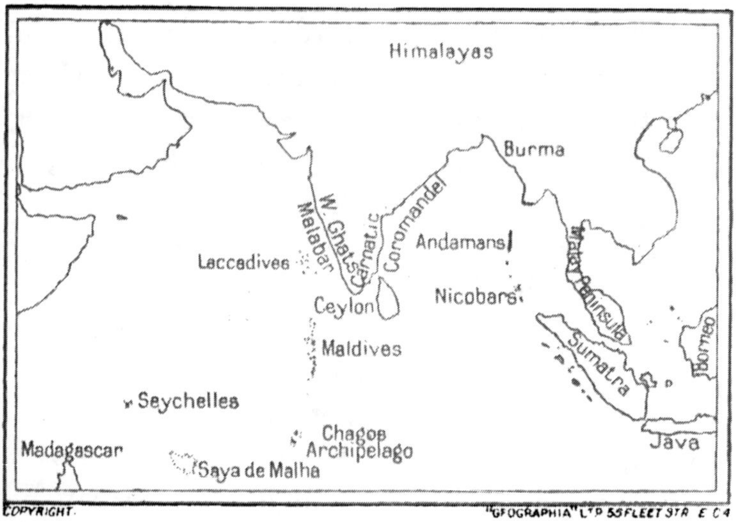


times a great island-continent, connected by a chain of islands—of which the Maldives, Chagos and Seychelles are a relic—with Madagascar and South Africa, and separated from the present heart of Asia by a deep channel—a channel perhaps traversed, much as now the West Indies traverse the Caribbean, by a series of islands, which may have been lowly precursors of the Himalayas: for those gigantic mountains are of comparatively recent origin."[1]

12. In this connection we have to keep in mind what was going on in other parts of Asia. The Andamans and Nicobars are peaks of a sunken range that rises again from the ocean both in Sumatra and in Western Burma. One of its secondary ridges is volcanic, and its continuation is to be found in the watershed separating the Irrawaddy and Sitang valleys.[2] The comparatively shallow sea to the east of this submarine range may, before it sank, have been in the nature of "brackish lakes extending well up into Burma, but while the northern part has since been raised, the central part has been depressed."[2] West of the Andaman ridge the ocean bed falls away to 2300 fathoms in the middle of the Bay of Bengal. Another arc of the Himalayas was raised up in a sweeping curve through the Peninsula and the Archipelago of Malaya. Borneo and Sumatra were frequently joined to and severed from the Asian Continent: but Java was finally cut off from it at an early date. Asia and Australia were irretrievably separated from each other by a vast ocean trench. Celebes was joined to neither, but was connected by the lost continent to Africa, and retains to this day

[1] *Spolia Zeylanica*, Vol. I, page 12.

[2] Journal, *Royal Geographical Society*, April, 1926, page 377.

the relic of a Miocene *fauna*.[1] We have therefore evidence of three land bridges from Southern Asia—one from South India and Ceylon towards Madagascar and South Africa : one from Western Burma through the Andamans to Sumatra : and one through the Malay Peninsula to Borneo.

13. With regard to the connection of Ceylon with Southern India, we must note that, in the zoological sense, the Indian Peninsula is divided into two geographical groups—that of the Malabar Coast, and that of the Central Provinces and the Carnatic. These two areas are separated from each other by the Western Ghats.

14. W. E. Wait, who has carefully studied the avifauna of Ceylon, suggests,[2] that the majority of the birds show an affinity with those of Malabar. This affinity applies specially to the highlands of the Kandyan Province and to the Wet Zone of the Low-country. On the other hand, in the extreme north and north-west of the Island the birds are largely the same as in the Carnatic, and of them several species and also several genera, do not occur either in the Malabar or in the wetter parts of Ceylon. By far the larger number of genera and species which are peculiar to Ceylon are, however, of the Malabar

[1] Enriquez' *Malaya*, Chapter II.
[2] Introduction : *Birds of Ceylon*.

type and have their habitat in the Wet Zone. Still more curious, is the fact that a few of the birds that are peculiar to Ceylon have their nearest relatives in the Himalayas or even in the Malay Archipelago, but none of them are of the Carnatic type. On the contrary, all the Himalayan species belong to Malabar types.

15. From these facts Wait suggests that the distribution of Ceylon birds can only be explained by assuming that the Malabar and Himalayan elements belong to an older period of contact between Ceylon and the Continent, when there was uninterrupted communication with the Malabar Coast. The Carnatic element, as we shall see, has not had time to evolve " peculiar " species, and is derived from a much later period.

16. In dating the earlier period of uninterrupted communication between Ceylon and Malabar, Wait thinks a clue may be found in the dozen Himalayan type birds now found in the Island. These include the Ceylon Magpie, two Hill Mynahs, Legge's Flower Pecker, the Yellow-fronted Barbet, the Broad-billed Roller, the Chestnut-headed Bee-eater, the Indian Edible-nest Swiftlet, the Frogmouth, the Ceylon Parroquet, the Ceylon Bay Owl, the Forest Eagle Owl, and the Bronze-winged Pigeon. Of all these, the nearest relatives are now found in the

Himalayas, a region which, as we have seen, has long been cut off by Gangetic seas or plains from Ceylon. But we know that at the close of the Tertiary Age glacial conditions rendered the climate of Northern Asia inhospitable, and the birds must, at that period, have been driven south. We have supposed that Ceylon was then joined to Malabar, and Himalayan birds, as well as those of Malabar, could thus have entered the Island. At least those of weak flight were subsequently cut off by a subsidence of the land-bridge when the approach of warmer conditions led to a general return migration northwards. Such a submergence of the land-bridge soon after the glacial epoch is indeed suggested by the fact that so many of the Himalayan type birds isolated in Ceylon are of weak flight. And in the long interval they have had time to become 'peculiar.' Such are the Yellow-fronted Barbet, the Ceylon Magpie, and Legge's Flower Pecker. Ceylon must then have remained an island for a very long geological period, for, out of the 360 species of birds recorded, no less than 49, or nearly one-seventh, are peculiar to the Island. The theory receives further support from the butterfly *Elymnias hypermnestra undularis* which occurs all over India except in the south, and appears again in Ceylon.[1]

[1] See Seitz' *Lepidoptera Indoaaustralica Diurna*, page 375.

17. Ceylon was rejoined to the Continent—and this time to the Carnatic—at a comparatively recent date. At this period occurred a second invasion—that of Carnatic birds, none of which have had time to evolve peculiar species. The dry-country Carnatic birds, which had hitherto been wanting in Ceylon, must have found, in the newly elevated sand tracts, a locality in which they could flourish: and, of course, the invasion would be accompanied by a good many birds too, which were common both to Malabar and to the Carnatic. This accounts for the fact that in so many Ceylonese families and genera, you will find a species which is strictly limited to the south-western region, living side by side with a new-comer whose distribution embraces the whole of Ceylon, Malabar, and the Carnatic.

18. Thus we see that, on the evidence of the birds, Ceylon must have been joined to India in Tertiary times, that it must have been isolated again for a very long period, and have been joined up once more for a short while at a recent date.

19. References are made in the *Mahawansa* to what appears to have been subsidences of land in historic times, a couple of centuries before the beginning of our era. It is mentioned that King Tissa was punished for some impiety by an encroachment of the sea. To propitiate the angry Spirits, he set

his daughter afloat in a canoe. This princess was rescued, and became the mother of King Dutthagamini. The settlement of the ancient aborigines at Lankapura is supposed to have been submerged, and it is possible that the earliest Sinhalese capitals, which have hitherto been sought for in vain, suffered a like fate.

20. At the present day a slow subsidence is in progress which, if continued, will result in another period of zoological isolation : but, as we have noted, the subsidences were never sufficiently profound to submerge the mountain ranges, and Ceylon does not appear to be subject to any violent seismic movements.

21. According to E. J. Wayland, the evidence of geology confirms, more or less, that of zoology.[1] Minor movements have oscillated the coast at various times, and are doubtless still in progress. Submerged pillars exist at Dondra below the high-tide level. But "whereas the most ancient movements which affected Ceylon were epeirogenic (or mountain-forming) in type, those of more recent date were orogenic (or continent-forming), that is, general and widespread in effect. . . . Some curious hydrographical phenomena, the facts of subterranean erosion, the rapid denudation of the coast, and the abrupt ending of shallow platforms under the sea, suggest that the land is now being slowly submerged."

[1] *Spolia Zeylanica,* Vol. X., page 266.

ANCIENT CEYLON

Graceful gestures in granite speak of a spiritual elation.

*Facing page 16*

## CHAPTER II

### HUMAN HISTORY OF CEYLON
### THE GREAT DYNASTY

22. Having noticed the Geological Romance of Ceylon, let us briefly survey its Human History, which extends far back into the mists of Time. Here again one is impressed with a sense of immense antiquity. In an age long previous to the most ancient legends, Man existed in Ceylon ; and, stone implements that have been found in caves and on hill-tops, seem to indicate that these early inhabitants were more or less contemporaneous with the Palæolithic people of Europe. Mr. Wayland thinks[1] there is nothing extravagant in the statement that Man was living in Ceylon a hundred thousand years ago.

23. Compared with such antiquity, the oldest of the legends that have accumulated through the centuries appear modern; yet they are amongst the most ancient of all human traditions, and stripped of extravagance they reveal the earliest known inhabitants as primitive Veddah tribes, such as those who still survive in Southern India, and in Ceylon itself. They are described for us by the first civilized

[1] *Spolia Zeylanica*, Vol. X, page 272.

immigrants as Rakshas (Demons) and Nagas (Snakes). Yet even these aborigines appear to have evolved some sort of organization, with a primitive settlement at the now vanished site of Lankapura. On the evidence of stone implements, Messrs. F. and P. Sarasin believe[1] that the present Veddahs are beings of a lower and older type than the other inhabitants of Ceylon—whether Tamil or Sinhalese—and that they must actually represent a remnant of the aborigines who were met with by the Sinhalese on their first arrival. "We maintain that the autochthony of the Veddahs of Ceylon is a proved fact : and further that the Sinhalese when they first came to the Island, already had iron, which they brought with them, and that this was taken over by the Veddahs in a relatively short time. . . . Thus we venture to say that the second main period of the Stone Age (the Neolithic), characterized by the polished stone axe, is entirely wanting in Ceylon, the Veddahs having made the step directly from the older (or Palæolithic) Stone Age to the modern age of iron."

24. According to the most ancient traditions, the site of Lankapura, together with other lands to the west of Ceylon, was submerged in the ocean at an early date. Indeed, Forbes believed that the name Lanka is the equivalent of Laka (million or multitude)

[1] *Spolia Zeylanica*, Vol. IV, page 188.

in Lakadives, 'The Numerous Islands,' which, according to the *Ramayana*, were once part of the Kingdom of Ravana.

25. Although the *Mahawansa* (to be mentioned later) must be regarded as the oldest record of authentic Sinhalese history, the Island under its Sanskrit name of 'Lanka' occupies a prominent place in the earlier mythical poetry of the Hindus. Very ancient references to it occur in Kashmir chronicles called the *Raja-Tarangini*: and its conquest by Rama is the theme of the *Ramayana* one of the world's oldest epics.[1]

26. The *Ramayana* relates the exile of Rama, telling how Sita was carried off by Ravana, the King of Lanka, and how Rama with his Ape-like allies rescued Sita and cast rocks and trees into the sea to make a causeway which, known to us as "Adam's Bridge," exists to this day. Sita Eliya (in the Nuwara Eliya District) is the place where Sita is supposed to have been imprisoned. These legends, which are thought to be about 4000 years old, may possibly refer to the earliest Aryan invasion of Ceylon. Such conquests, however, were of a quite temporary nature. Authentic history only begins with the landing of Vijaya in 543 B.C. This event has no doubt been antedated to some extent by early chronologists in their

[1] Tennent's *Ceylon*, page 315, note 1.

anxiety to make Vijaya a contemporary of the Buddha.

27. Vijaya, an Aryan, half bandit, half prince, came from the mainland with seven hundred followers, and married a Veddah chieftainess called Kuwani. After Kuwani had betrayed her country and her people for love of him, she was deserted, together with her children. She returned to her own folk and was slain. Vijaya built a primitive settlement at Tamana Nuwara, and founded a Sinhalese dynasty that was destined to survive for nearly eight centuries. The earliest capitals were at Tambupani and Upatissagama, but the site of neither has yet been discovered. These early Sinhalese of the Sinha, or 'Lion Race,' brought with them a considerable civilization. The beginnings of great irrigation works, which afterwards became a feature of their administration, were opened near Anuradhapura by the successors of Vijaya in about 504 B.C. The irrigation works no doubt produced and encouraged a considerable population, and these early centuries of social achievement have to be regarded as the well-laid foundation upon which, with amazing suddenness, a brilliant culture was soon to rise.

28. To this budding and receptive civilization, the introduction of Buddhism in the third century B.C. proved an event of tremendous consequence, supplying

as it did an impetus and an inspiration. It is to the *Mahawansa* that we owe the record of these incidents: and it is to Tournour, an officer of the Ceylon Civil Service, that we owe the discovery (in 1826) of the *Mahawansa.* The scholarly research of Turnour inspired Tennent's *Ceylon,* a standard work to which all subsequent writers are deeply indebted. The *Mahawansa,* says Tennent, "is a metrical chronicle, containing a dynastic history of Ceylon from 543 B.C. to A.D. 1758. Being written in Pali verse, its existence in modern times was only known to the priests: and owing to the obscurity of its diction it had ceased to be studied by even the learned amongst them. . . . Pali authors of antiquity were accustomed to accompany their metrical compositions with a 'tika' or running commentary, which contained a literal version of the mystical text, and supplied illustrations of its more abstruse passages." Such a 'Tika' on the *Mahawansa* was generally known to have been written. Knox, whose *History of Ceylon* was published in 1817, says that "The Sinhalese possess some written and some traditional narratives of their primitive history which are not undeserving of attention": and Valentyne who "exhibited a copious list of Sinhalese Kings," evidently had access, directly or indirectly, to old manuscripts.[1] But so utterly had the *Maha-*

[1] Knox's *History of Ceylon,* page 17.

*wansa* been neglected, that Turnour till 1826 had never met with an individual who had critically read the text, or more than casually heard of the existence of the 'tika.' At length, amongst books supplied to him by the high priest of Saffaragam, was one which proved to be the lost commentary on the mystic and otherwise unintelligible *Mahawansa*. Such is the romantic tale of the salvage of Sinhalese History from obscurity.

29. Tennent says: "The title *Mahawansa*, which means literally the 'genealogy of the great,' properly belongs to the first section of the work, extending from 543 B.C. to A.D. 301, and containing the history of the early kings, from Vijaya (or Wijayo) to Maha Sen with whom the Sinhalese consider the 'Great Dynasty' to end. The author of this portion was Mahanamo, uncle of King Dhatu Sen, in whose reign it was compiled between the years A.D. 459 and 477 from annals in the vernacular language then existing in Anarajapoora. . . . The sovereigns who succeeded Maha Sen are distinguished as the 'Sulawansa,' or 'Lower race,' and the story of their line occupied the continuation of this extraordinary chronicle, the second portion of which was written by order of the illustrious King Prakrama Bahu about the year A.D. 1266. The narrative was carried on under subsequent sovereigns down to the year A.D.

1758." Such are the sources from which the ancient history of Ceylon has been recovered.

30. The fact that the Sinhalese themselves spoke a Pali language related to Sanskrit may account for the instant success of the Buddhist Mission sent to Ceylon by Asoka in charge of his son Mahinda. Whatever the cause of the ready acceptance of the new religion, the effect of its mild and benevolent influence was magical. In India itself, the culture of the Greeks meeting with that of Buddhism and mingling with it, had produced an inspiration to which we owe the classic Græco-Buddhist statuary of Gandhara. With this spirit of benevolent enthusiasm, the Magadhan States of Northern India reached their zenith under the humane and lovable Asoka. His contemporary in Ceylon was King Tissa.

31. To Tissa, Asoka sent tidings of Buddhism in 307 B.C by the mouth of his son Mahinda. The direct results of that Mission are the monuments of Mahintale and Anuradhapura, whose ruins, even after a lapse of two thousand years, are still amongst the wonders of the world. As Tennent has pointed out, modifications of those hemispherical masses of brick "may be traced in every Buddhist country of Asia, in the *topes* of Afghanistan and the Punjab, in the pagodas of Burma, and in the Boro Bodeo of Java." They are, in fact, the prototype of the universal

pagoda, just as the Buddha figure of ancient Gandhara was the prototype of all the Buddhas in Asia from Peshawar to Yokohama. The very word 'pagoda' is a corruption of 'dagaba' or 'dagoba,' from *Datu* (a relic) and *gabbhan* (a shrine).

32. The meeting of Tissa and Mahinda on the site of what is now Manintale (eight miles from Anuradhapura) is described vividly in the *Mahawansa*. Mahinda delivered his message thus: "We are the ministers and disciples of the Lord of the true faith: and in compassion for thee, Maharajah, we have repaired hither." The rocky hill now called Mahintale is the impressive monument of Mahinda and of the successful Mission. Upon it was erected a vast 'vihara,' or monastery, to commemorate the conversion of Tissa. The ashes of Mahinda himself are enshrined in the Ambustela Dagoba which, according to tradition, marks the very spot of his meeting with Tissa. These buildings were added to by succeeding monarchs.

33. The zeal of King Tissa led to the erection of many other great monuments at Anuradhapura, where, in imitation of King Bimbisara's gift of a garden to the Buddha, Tissa made a present to the religion of his pleasure grounds at Mahamegha. This garden is twenty square miles in extent, and adjoined the then royal city of Anuradhapura. The

Thuparama Pagoda was the first building tobe erected in 307 B.C. Cave says : " This monument is in itself evidence of the remarkable skill of architect, builder and sculptor in Ceylon at a period anterior to that of any existing monument on the mainland." Like all Sinhalese dagobas, it is bell-shaped. Tennent points out that the great interest of the Thuparama Pagoda, the first of all Sinhalese monuments, is that " in all probability it is the oldest architectural monument now extant in India." And, he adds, " In elegance of outline it immeasurably surpassed all the other dagobas. The beauty of its design is still perceptible in its ruin after a lapse of two thousand years."

34. But here a word of caution is necessary. It is now evident that we have no means of ascertaining what restorations have been made in the course of centuries. It is established that mediæval restorers had as little historic sense as modern ones ; but on the other hand they had not (fortunately) the imagination to depart from stereotyped forms.

35. The sacred Bo Tree is probably the best known of all the wonders of Anuradhapura. The venerable tree is directly associated with Mahinda himself across the intervening gulf of two millenniums. The enthusiasm of the new converts was such, that a nun was required to take the vows of the women. To meet this emergency, Mahinda summoned his own sister,

Sanghamitta ; and by her hand Asoka (in about 288 B.C.) sent a branch of the actual Bo Tree under which the Lord Buddha had attained 'Enlightment.' This tree still survives at Anuradhapura, and is, therefore, a living link with the 'Blessed One' himself. "Endowed," says the *Mahawansa,* "with many miraculous powers, it has stood for ages in the delightful Mahamegha Garden in Lanka, promoting the spiritual welfare of the inhabitants and the propagation of the true religion."

36. Another ancient shrine on this site attributed to King Tissa is the Isuru-muniya Temple—a curious monument built into the natural rock, and occupying a romantic situation beside a lake. It was only rediscovered in the middle of the last century, for it must be remembered that until the Archæological Department of the British Government took over the site, all these monuments were overgrown with thick jungle, and many were completely lost. It is difficult now to realize this, or to give the praise that is due to the Archæological Department, when one sees only beautiful park-like country on all sides, with innumerable baths, pillars, plynths, tanks, statues, frescoes, and monoliths scattered about over the turf-land.

37. Unfortunately, even the initial wave of Buddhist enthusiasm was checked by an invasion of Tamils.

This was by no means the first of such visitations. The earliest known Tamil eruption occurred in about 237 B.C. Ceylon was not the only country afflicted at this period by invasions from Southern India. Lower Burma, then in possession of the Talaings, was faced with similar troubles at the beginning of the Christian era, when adventurous and aggressive Cholas swarmed across the Bay, and formed colonies at Thaton and Bassein. In fact the word Talaing, which has ever since been applied to the Mongolian race of Mon, is probably derived from the Talingana country of Southern India.

38. The Indian invasion of Ceylon, that we are now considering, was headed by Elara or Elala. He was a Chola, a native of Tanjore, and he ruled with considerable strength and justice for no less than forty years. His memory is still fresh: and his death, after a personal combat with King Dutthagamini in A.D. 161, supplies Sinhalese history with its one note of chivalry. The victorious Sinhalese king erected a magnificent tomb over the remains of his foreign rival, and the combat is commemorated in a fresco in the Cave Temple of Dambulla.

39. "In the epics of Buddhism," says Tennent, "Dutthagamini enjoys a renown second only to that of Tissa as a champion of the faith." He quickly restored the country to peace and prosperity. The

number of monks soon increased enormously, and for their accommodation he built a vast monastery, the Maha-Lowa-Paya, or Loha Pasada, now known as the 'Brazen Palace,' because originally it was roofed with plates of metal. This extraordinary building rested on a forest of 1600 granite columns, and these are now all that remain. The richly decorated superstructure of nine stories has disappeared: and indeed part of it was pulled down in the very next reign to furnish material for rival monasteries at a period when a dissension threatened the unity of the Buddhist Church. The 'Brazen Palace' was being frequently pulled down and restored up till the 12th century.

40. A more enduring monument of Dutthagamini is the Ruanweli, or Gold-dust Pagoda. "The new religion," says Cave, "had filled its votaries with almost superhuman energy, and only the very hills themselves could compare with the buildings which were the outward expression of their devotion. Foundations were laid to a depth of one hundred feet, and composed of layers of crystallized stone, and plates of iron and copper: and upon such basements were piled millions of tons of masonry. We see the remains of one of these stupendous edifices in the Ruanweli. Its present appearance is that of a conical hill nearly 200 feet high, covered with

trees, and surmounted by a small spire. It is, however, a mass of solid brickwork. Time, and the frequent attacks of enemies, have to a great extent obliterated the original design: but there is sufficient of the structure still remaining to verify the accounts of ancient writers who have transmitted to us full details of the building as it was erected in the second century B.C. We should not believe those accounts without the evidence of the ruins." The lower part of the Ruanweli Dagoba has now been restored.

41. "From the lowest platform rises another, an immense square measuring 500 feet each way, and made to appear as if supported on about four hundred elephants. These elephants (now sadly ruined) form a retaining wall. They are modelled in brick, and are placed less than two feet apart. . . . The platform furnishes a foundation to sustain the ponderous mass of the solid brick shrine which was built upon it to a height of 270 feet, and with an equal diameter at the base of the dome."

42. The ruins of baths and reservoirs are outstanding features of the old sites. They are known locally as 'pokunas.' It must be remembered that the ancient prosperity of Ceylon arose from irrigation works, that were undertaken at an early date. Nearly all the lakes which still exist are artificial, and they formed part of a wide system of waterways. The decay

of these works resulted immediately in the impoverishment and ruin of the country: and these miseries continued until the beginning of the last century when the British Government began to restore the old sluices and embankments. At that time the inhabitants of the interior had reached the lowest ebb of misfortune and disease. Their restoration to peace and plenty is the direct result of the Government's labours. The three great lakes at Anuradhapura, were a part of this ancient system, and furnished the Royal City with water for drinking, washing, and for ceremonial bathing. "We cannot help reflecting," says Cave in his *Ruined Cities of Ceylon*, "that the famous baths of Roman emperors were constructed contemporaneously with these, and that while those of Caracalla and Diocletian, being built of brick, have crumbled now beyond repair, the picturesque and elegant baths of Dutthagamini, with their beautiful terraces and granite stairs, can, with little trouble, be restored to their pristine condition. . . . There is something very impressive about these remnants of ancient luxury hidden in the lonely forest."

43. Dutthagamini died in 137 B.C., and thirty years later the Tamil menace returned. King Walagam Bahu was deposed, and for fifteen years the destroying foreigner possessed the land. It was at this distressful

period that Walagam Bahu used the caverns at Dambulla as a refuge. Upon his restoration he converted them into the great 'Cave Temple' that is a popular object of pilgrimage to this day. Eventually Walagam Bahu drove the Tamils away and reoccupied his throne: and, nothing daunted by his late misfortunes, proceeded to build monuments which should eclipse even the ambitious works of his predecessors. Amongst these was the Abhayagiri Dagoba, now distinguished by the name of 'Northern Stupa.' It is one of the greatest pagodas in the world and is believed to have attained a height of 450 feet. That is, it was fifty feet higher than St. Paul's! The superstructure is now seriously ruined, but the shrine still covers an area of eight acres.

44. A more useful achievement of this reign was the convocation of a Buddhist Assembly in the 1st century B.C. at which, not only were the existing disputes and heresies discussed, but the sayings of Buddha were committed to writing for the first time. This important work, of such particular interest to all Buddhists, was carried out at what is now known as the Rock Temple of Alu-wihare near Matale.

45. We have mentioned that the Buddhist Church was rent by a heresy. King Maha Sen (A.D. 275–302) adopted it, and hundreds of monasteries, including the Brazen Palace, were destroyed to furnish materials

for the monuments of the new sect. But serious discontent ensued, and eventually, perhaps for political reasons, Maha Sen reverted to the faith of his fathers. The ruins which we have now to consider belong to this period. The greatest of them is the Jetawanarama, or 'Eastern Pagoda,' which is attributed to the middle of Maha Sen's reign, just before his return to pure religion. The building was completed in the time of his son Kitsiri Maiwan. The following is Sir Emerson Tennent's remark upon this gigantic monument. True, it should have been written of the Abhayagiri, for, as explained later, the identity of the two stupas has been confused : but they are so alike that the description may stand : "Its diameter is 360 feet, and its present height, including pedestal and spire, 249 feet : so that the contents of the semicircular dome of brickwork and the platform of stone 720 feet square and 15 feet high, exceed 20 million cubic feet. . . . The materials are sufficient to raise eight thousand houses, each with twenty feet frontage, and these would form thirty streets half a mile in length. The bricks would construct a town the size of Ipswich or Coventry ; they would line an ordinary railway tunnel twenty miles long, or form a wall one foot thick and twenty feet high, reaching from London to Edinburgh. Such are the dagobas of Anuradhapura —structures whose stupendous dimensions, and the waste and misapplication of labour lavished on them, are hardly outdone even in the instance of the Pyramids of Egypt." The study of these activities explains how it was that, in the early centuries of our era, Ceylon had the energy to influence distant countries, and to spread her culture and religion to Burma, Java and even to far Siam.

46. It is not easy to comprehend how the ancient Sinhalese kings achieved this notable civilization unless we study their methods of government. "The patriarchal village system," says Tennent, "which from time immemorial has been one of the characteristics of the Dekkan, and which still prevails throughout Ceylon in a modified form, was one of the first institutions organized by the successors of Vijaya. . . . Upwards of two hundred years were spent in initiatory measures for the organization of the new state, and colonists from the continent of India were encouraged." In addition, the great irrigation system had produced a large population, and there was considerable trade—notably in precious stones—with many distant countries. Knox[1] says that in the 6th century Ceylon was used as a port-of-call by vessels sailing to the East, and that its merchants received silk, aloes, and sandalwood from China, and pepper from India. Strabo mentions that Taprobane supplied the Indian

[1] Knox's *History of Ceylon*, page 6.

markets with ivory and tortoise-shell. Ceylon, therefore, was evidently not completely isolated from the world. It was wealthy, and the Government had the will and the power to press its subjects into service. Mention is occasionally made of paid labour: but it seems that the peasantry held their land under the obligation to render service. It was out of their sweat and toil that vast pagodas and other public works were accomplished. But, however arduous this forced labour may have been, it must be admitted that the irrigation system at any rate was for the people's good; and when it fell into neglect, and when the power of the Great Dynasty waned, poverty and disease quickly reduced the splendour of Ceylon to ghastly ruin.

47. Maha Sen died in A.D. 302. He is the last of those referred to as of the *Mahawansa*, or "Great Dynasty."

. . . . .

48. This early Ceylon was not entirely unknown to Europe. Ptolemy imagined the country to be part of a continent. He wrote of Anuradhapura under the name of 'Anurogrammum Regium,' and his map of the country dates from A.D. 150[1]. "India's utmost Isle" is mentioned by Ovid as a place

[1] E. Reimers, *Ceylon Daily News*, of 6th June, 1927; and Tennent's *Ceylon*, Vol. II, page 611.

incredibly remote. According to Pliny, it was not understood to be an island until the time of Alexander. In the reign of Claudius, a Roman, Annius Plocamus, was blown to Ceylon by a storm, and there resided six months. His visit resulted in a Sinhalese embassy to Rome.[1]

49. Knox considers that Pliny's account shows Ceylon to have had "a greater degree of civil liberty, and a greater regard for popular rights, than perhaps ever existed in any region of the East."

50. Then the veil of mediæval darkness falls, and we hear no more from Europe, until Marco Polo's visit late in the 13th century. By that time, even Ceylon had long since forgotten her former glories.

[1] Knox's *History of Ceylon*, Chapter I.

## CHAPTER III

## HUMAN HISTORY OF CEYLON
## THE LESSER DYNASTIES

51. In the last chapter, we have followed the destinies of Ceylon through the period of its splendour, and up to the close of the 'Great Dynasty' at the death of King Maha Sen in A.D. 302.

52. It was in the reign of his son, Kitsiri Maiwan, that the 'Tooth Relic,' or 'Dalada,' came to Ceylon in A.D. 311. The relic is said to have been brought by a fugitive Indian Princess who carried it hidden in her hair. Pagodas called Dalada Maligawa were built at Anuradhapura and afterwards at Polonnaruwa for its reception. The Tooth was more than once removed for safety at times of Tamil invasion, but it was carried off by them to India in the 14th century. Subsequently, the Sinhalese bought it back. Eventually, as we shall see, it was destroyed by the Portuguese, though the natives are still satisfied that the original relic survives at Kandy, where a substitute continues to be an object of veneration. It is curious to note that the obviously spurious relic of Ceylon is passionately believed in as genuine, while the Peshawar relic (now in Mandalay), of whose authenticity there is

SIGIRIYA

This impregnable rock was converted into a fortress by the parricide King, Kassiyappa, in the fifth century. From its summit he ruled Ceylon for 18 years.

not a shadow of doubt, has never achieved any real popularity. For centuries, Burma has accepted counterfeits with pathetic eagerness. Now that an authentic relic has come unexpectedly into her possession, Burma does not believe. Perhaps the times are gone when teeth and white elephants had a superlative value.

53. We have briefly noticed a few of the monuments at Anuradhapura—but only a few. Hundreds more lie scattered over the site ; and minor ones may still remain buried in the jungle. But now the scene shifts to Sigiriya.

54. Sigiriya is a rock fortress, founded in the middle of the 5th century by the parricide prince Kassiyappa, after he had murdered his father Datu Sen in A.D. 477. Kassiyappa was overthrown by his brother eighteen years later : but after a long series of dynastic quarrels Anuradhapura was finally abandoned in A.D. 769.

55. The occupation of Sigiriya therefore marks the decline of Sinhalese greatness. The hill, which was now converted into a fortress, is a mass of gneiss with precipitous walls. It was only approachable by means of stone galleries which have since been restored. Some minor ruins and frescoes survive at the summit : but by this time Art in Ceylon had passed the zenith of its glory. After the final

abandonment of Anuradhapura, a new capital grew up at Polonnaruwa.

56. Cave says: "Polonnaruwa had been a place of royal residence in the palmiest days of the old city, but it was not till the 8th century that it was adopted as the seat of Government. The decay of Anuradhapura had been creeping on ever since the days of Kassiyappa and the fortification of Sīgiriya. Internecine war, fostered by rival branches of the royal house, no less than the interminable struggle with Tamil invaders, hastened its downfall. The history of the 6th and 7th centuries is a story of bloodshed and anarchy. Wholesale emigration set it, cultivation was interrupted, and buildings and irrigation works alike were destroyed or neglected." At length, in the 10th century, the Tamils, or Cholas, under their King Rajaraja, taking advantage of the internal dissension of the Sinhalese, so strengthened their position in and round Anuradhapura that the only means by which the Sinhalese government could retain any pretence of power lay in retiring. "These circumstances led to the establishment of Polonnaruwa as the capital, and the fate of Anuradhapura was sealed, for when abandoned to the Tamils, its debasement and ruin were assured."

57. "That the Sinhalese (at Polonnaruwa), should have been able, notwithstanding this constant

disquiet, to build and maintain another city of such notable wealth and beauty is proof enough of the splendid qualities of the race."

58. This unexpected revival was achieved by Vijaya Bahu I in A.D. 1071. The period was one of vigorous resistance to the Indians in several countries. The growth of their power was probably the real cause of King Anawratta's sudden descent on Lower Burma in A.D. 1057. His better-known sack of the Talaing capital of Thaton was probably incidental. In Burma we do not hear of another war-like invasion by southern Indians, but their peaceful penetration continues to cause alarm to this day ; and as Northern Ceylon is now largely Indian so also is southern Burma.

59. Under Vijaya Bahu's successor, the national hero Prakrama Bahu I (A.D. 1155–80), the Indian menace in Ceylon was again temporarily checked. Not only did Prakrama regain possession of the whole Island, but he even invaded India. Having subdued his enemies, he repaired the irrigation works, and in many ways relieved and comforted his broken people. Disputes and heresies were calmed by his skill and tact, and also, one suspects, by more forceful kinds of persuasion too. Buddhism, which had nearly disappeared during the late troubles, was restored. Alms houses and hospitals were established : and then

Prakrama set out to embellish Polonnaruwa on a scale calculated even to rival the old capital. He surrounded the city with a mighty wall, and built many beautiful and interesting shrines. Such were the Jetawana-rama, the Thuparama, and the curious rock-cut temple of Gal-wihara with its colossal hewn figures. Other important monuments are the Sat-mahal pasada, and the Dalada Maligawa : but it is not certain to whom they should be attributed. There is a strong Hindu element mixed with the Buddhism of Polonnaruwa. Owing to the decline of Sinhalese art during the preceding wars, Indian architects and sculptors were imported. The two Siva Devale temples are frankly Hindu. Unfortunately, this part of Sinhalese achievement lasted only a century. After reigning thirty-three years, the great and magnificent Prakrama died in A.D. 1172. A dozen successors were murdered, blinded or deposed in quick succession. In 1215 twenty thousand destroying Tamils poured over the land : and in this torrent the Sinhalese were irretrievably submerged. So they fell into degradation and decay after a history that has been ranked, not unjustly, with that of Babylon.

60. How unstable the Sinhalese Governments really were, at least in later times, may be judged from the fact that, of the Kings who ruled between 307 B.C.

THUPARAMA (POLONNARUWA)

Hindu influence is strong in the architecture of the second capital. Sinhalese art had suffered in the late wars.

Facing page 40

and A.D. 1815, "fifteen reigned less than a year and thirty others less than two years : twenty-two were murdered by their successors, and six by other individuals : thirteen fell in war and feuds : and eleven were dethroned."[1] Not only that, but the great men who have been mentioned here are the only ones who appeared. They stand isolated in a mediocrity, incapacity and selfishness that continued without relief for two thousand years.

[1] Turnour.

## CHAPTER IV

## MAHINTALE

(The Age of Mahinda)

61. Of all ancient sites, Anuradhapura alone has preserved unbroken a Buddhist record from the days of Asoka until our own. So much of romance, such great and beautiful monuments, such intricate history, and above all an antiquity so tremendous, are positively staggering. Its oldest lake, the Basawak Kalama, was constructed five centuries before the birth of Christ. Its oldest pagoda, the Thuparama, built in B.C. 307, is not only the most ancient monument in Ceylon, but the oldest surviving building in the whole of India. And here grows the oldest historic tree in the world, the subject of hoary legends. Yet, thanks to the *Mahawansa*, a wealth of detail survives. The approximate dates of many ruins, the story of their inception, the history of their construction, are preserved : and in addition to these cold facts, there remain pictures of individuals, and piquant touches of human nature, that make the dead generations live for us again.

62. The word 'Anuradhapura' does not mean 'City of Ninety Kings,' as is popularly supposed.

It is derived from *Anuradha*, a certain constellation of stars, under which the city was founded. The site is said to have been chosen by King Pandukabhaya in 457 B.C., though it did not become the seat of Government till a century later. With the exception of a brief interlude in favour of Sigiriya, it remained the capital of Ceylon until finally abandoned in A.D. 769.

63. The early history of Ceylon is so closely connected with its monuments, that it is impossible to tell it without reference to them: and the first to be considered are those at Mahintale, 8 miles distant from Anuradhapura. They come first because they are associated with those earliest events which, in 307 B.C., led immediately to the rise of Sinhalese culture—namely, the advent of Mahinda, the Apostle of Buddhism, sent to Ceylon by his father, King Asoka. Mahinda on his arrival at the capital found King Tissa absent, and proceeded to follow him. The meeting took place on the hill that has since been called Mahintale after the illustrious missionary: and it was here that he spoke those memorable words: "In compassion for thee, Maharajah, we have repaired hither."

64. Tennent considers that Mahintale is the oldest place of mountain pilgrimage in Ceylon—older even than Adam's Peak. A litter of ruins bespeaks the

reverence with which the site was regarded from the earliest times. The ancient pagodas that adorn the hill are monuments to Mahinda himself. Here also he died. The very road by which the hill is approached is full of associations with the Great Ones of the first Dynasty. The base of the hill is crowded with such ruins as the Kaludiva Cave, Rajagiri-lena where stone steps lead to a cell amidst a titanic pile of rocks, and the Indikatusaya Tope of which the lower part is built of solid stone. Indikatusaya is interesting because it is supposed to have been 'elongated,' or 'drum shaped,'[1] like the archaic pagodas of Prome in Burma. Little of its brick superstructure, however, remains.

65. Mahintale is a lone group of hills rising out of the plain to a height of about a thousand feet. The main peak is ascended by a stairway of more than a thousand granite blocks. It is one of the wonders of Ceylon. These steps, and the massive stones of which they are composed, testify to the fact that we are dealing with the work of giants rather than of men; and the same idea recurs all the way up where, on every level space, granite monoliths are scattered about—here a great canoe-shaped trough, there pillars and gigantic inscribed tablets. These last date from the 10th century A.D. But Sinhalese was written

[1] *Ceylon Journal of Science*, Vol. I, Part III, page 1.

in Asokan characters at a very early date—probably 200 B.C., though there is a curious gap in the inscriptions from about the 6th to the 8th century. Pali script came later. The very lengthy inscriptions of Anurádhapura and Polonnaruwa, like these at Mahintale, are usually 10th century or later.

66. The most pleasing of all these monuments is the Lion Bath, a picturesque little reservoir from whose side issues a splendid rampant lion. This is really a very fine composition, and one of the most interesting works at Mahintale from the artistic point of view.

67. The hill itself is pleasantly wooded, the turf beneath the trees being scattered over with a confusion of boulders. Up these slopes the steps ascend, till at last you reach the Ambustela Dagoba that nestles in a fold of the mountain just below the summit. This is a very ancient monument, built to mark the place where Mahínda and King Tissa met. According to the legend, Tissa, who was out hunting, was lured to the spot by a Goddess in the guise of a deer. The ashes of Mahinda are said to be enshrined in the Ambustella Dagoba. Slender stone pillars encircle the shrine, which slumbers peacefully in the shade of coco-nut palms. Indeed, there are rather too many palms, for they impede the view. A few yards away, on the actual summit of the mountain, rises

an ancient brick tope—the Etwihara Dagoba—which is supposed to enshrine a hair of the Buddha. It dates from the very beginning of our era, and is now much ruined. This summit is referred to in Buddhist literature as Ambatthalo. The view is superb. On one side you look down upon the lakes and monuments of Anuradhapura, and on the other across the plain with its green tree-tops spreading unbroken to distant peaks that are strung along the horizon. It is indeed a lovely spot, that has inspired men since ancient days : for its natural beauty is enhanced by the old-world legend of Mahinda, and by the fact that here, on this mountain-top, occurred events that were destined to leave an indelible mark on the history of the Oriental World. In India Buddhism soon died out : but in Ceylon it survived, and was to spread thence throughout Eastern Asia.

68. In the foreground of this view, rises a bold pinnacle of rock known as 'Mahinda's Couch,' upon which the Apostle is supposed to have alighted, and upon which he used to meditate. Would it be possible to find a spot more contemplative? The point of naked rock rises high above the tree-tops, breasting the plain, whose dark foliage spreads away into the distance like a sea.

CHAPTER V

# ANURADHAPURA

## (The First Great Capital)

69. We have now to return to Anuradhapura. The question is often asked—" Can it be seen in a day ? " The reply is that emphatically it cannot, but that it frequently is. Nevertheless, its charms are not for those who hurry by. It is a place to linger over. We must get into harmony with its antiquity : we must absorb its atmosphere of history and romance. The thoughtful student will find many things to weigh and ponder ; for these ancient stones, apparently so uniform, possess in fact an endless individuality. New impressions crowd in upon one, and they thicken as one begins to appreciate the significance of the many problems presented. I can truly say that an Author is to be pitied who sets out to reduce Anuradhapura to ordered writing. It is indeed a tremendous task.

70. The site of the ruins lies roughly north and south ; but it is rambling, and its topography difficult to grasp. Still, the monuments resolve themselves into groups, and we will begin with the central one —firstly, because it *is* central, and secondly, because

it is the least attractive on account of its proximity to the modern town. Here the ruins lie cheek by jowl with offices and bungalows, and lose something of their romance by the intrusion of the bazaar. True, it is not an extensive bazaar, but the Brazen Palace and the Bo Tree are right in it, and it disturbs their repose. Humanity is all very well. God made even guides and beggars. But Man improves with distance, and he becomes even romantic down a vista of two thousand years, which is his proper place here.

71. Do we truly read those ancients, I wonder, down that long long trail? By their works only we must judge them: and surely, it must be that—in spite of their roughness of their age—they were men of simple heart and childish piety—Tissa, Mahinda, Dutthagamini and the rest. I picture them as essentially gentlemen: at least there was nothing small or petty about them. Surely they were men of character. Certain it is that they possessed a tremendous energy, and that they were inspired by a high ideal. Nevertheless, new Anuradhapura is probably more comfortable than old. How awful to have to wait—as in mediæval Mandalay—perhaps three months in hourly expectation of a summons to the 'Golden Feet.'

72. There is, however, one modern type that is in harmony with the stage—the Buddhist Pilgrim. The

Sinhalese are great pilgrims—lovers of picnic like the Burmese: and these happy parties are frankly and joyously appreciative of all things quaint and wonderful, as good Buddhists should be, and as their ancestors were, who soon exhausted all the most impossible sites on peak and rock, and were reduced to building on the ground like ordinary mortals. Like ourselves, these pilgrims are out to enjoy the grotesque, the unusual, the marvellous. *Thadu! Thadu!*

73. The Bo Tree is essentially a thing one would have preferred to see without sordid disturbances. Here is the oldest historic tree in the world—a living link with good King Asoka—nay, a living link with the Buddha himself. Fa Hien has gazed upon it reverently. There may exist trees that are older, but none have such beautiful associations, and none are so well attested and documented. The Bo Tree may have been a branch of the very tree under which The Master won 'Enlightenment,' it probably was; but in any case it is now so venerable that it has achieved sanctity on its own account. From ancient times Kings and Princes have fenced it about with heavy walls and platforms that still remain, and have enriched its neighbourhood with works of art.

74. The Bo Tree, as we have seen, was brought over to Ceylon by Sanghamitta, the sister of Mahinda,

in 288 B.C., nineteen years after Tissa's conversion: so that it is now not less than 2215 years old: and throughout those two millenniums it has been guarded, cared for and revered, and its vicissitudes minutely recorded, so that its death is a thing almost unthinkable. Yet, evidently, dissolution is not far off. The tree is only half the size it was seventy years ago, to judge by Tennent's sketch.[1] Now only two branches remain, and neither of them is robust—proof positive, in 'reformed' political circles, of the extreme wickedness of the British Government! And it is the British Government which, alone of all Governments, has cared for and cherished the monuments of ancient Ceylon. Was there ever such base ingratitude? As a matter of fact gratitude is purely an individual quality. There is no such thing as gratitude in masses.

75. The leaves of the sacred tree are most carefully preserved, though it is to be feared there are not enough for all the pilgrims. Fortunately, however, leaves do not only grow on this one tree. But having is believing; and I am assured by irrefutable authorities that my own leaf is genuine.

76. The Bo Tree, or to give it its full title, the *Jaya Sri Maha Bodin—Wahanse*[2] (the Victorious, Illustrious Supreme Lord, the Sacred Bo Tree),

[1] Tennent's *Ceylon*, Vol. II, page 614.
[2] Tennent's *Ceylon*, Vol. II, page 613.

stands now on a high plinth, jealously guarded by a railing. Of the objects round about its shaded court, the most interesting are some old Buddhas, and the 'Moon Stone' at the foot of the steps. This last, though often praised, and figured in Tennent's *Ceylon* (Vol. II, page 619), is by no means the finest 'Moon Stone' in Anuradhapura. The outer walls of the enclosure are evidently of great antiquity.

77. Close to the Bo Tree is the Brazen Palace, called Maha-lowa-paya. It is the ruin of that famous seven-storied monastery built by Dutthagamini. It has been described so often that it will suffice to say that what survives (evidently only the supports on which the building rested) is a perfect forest of stone pillars, each eight or ten feet high, packed close, and covering several acres of ground. Amongst other curious monuments in this central group are two baths, popularly known as the King's Bath and the Queen's Bath: and a ruin near the post office which possesses one of those extraordinary canoe-shaped troughs which will be referred to again later. Lastly, there is the Ruanweli Dagoba.

78. Ruanweli (King Dutthagamini: 137 B.C.) is one of the three gigantic stupas of Anuradhapura. It has suffered a merciless restoration, its walls having been rebuilt to a height of over a hundred feet. The summit is still overgrown with shrubs, but in Tennent's

day the whole pagoda was covered with great trees that were tearing it to pieces. Originally the court that surrounds it was supported by a noble fresco of elephants but this fresco is now much ruined. The *Mahawansa* mentions a restoration in A.D. 246 when a glass spire was erected "to serve as a protection against lightning." Forbes has pointed out (page 224) the interest of this early appreciation of the non-conducting qualities of glass. The circular brick walls of the tope rise from three low plinths, and swell upwards like a mighty globe. It is this upward bellying that has now been restored. The summit of the pagoda is still a shapeless mass of debris. Close up, the building looks dull and meaningless by reason of its unrelieved surface of brick. To view it to advantage, and to appreciate the soaring effect of its curving walls, one must stand well back till it is seen rising splendidly over the tree-tops: and it is not difficult to place in the foreground of the picture a clump of slender pillars, for the neighbourhood is scattered about with the minor ruins of monastic halls. Thus seen, Ruanweli achieves dignity, and the modern atrocities that cluster round its base, like ugly little bugs, are decently hidden.

79. It is typical of the frivolous 'reformed' Government of to-day that, while fussing about immaterial things, it should still permit ignorant people to mutilate

Ruanweli Pagoda. B.C. 137.
By King Dutthagimini

THUPARAMA. By King Tissa. B.C. 307.
This is the oldest surviving monument in Ceylon or India

ANURADHAPURA

The first capital of Ceylon. 3rd Century B.C. to A.D. 729.

*Facing page 52*

their public monuments with horrid and meaningless additions. The theory is that the monuments belong to the people and not to the Archæological Department, as if the Department was not the servant of the Public, and the proper guardian of its treasures. Such an attitude may be incomprehensible in England, where Services like the Police, and so on, are regarded as the Friends of the People, and not its Enemies. In the East it is different ; and education will have to go deeper before people can be made to see the sacrilege of roofing with tin plates a building two thousand years old, and painting it an excruciating blue. Meanwhile one can only regret that a very laudable desire to contribute pavilions and altars cannot be just as well satisfied by the re-erection of any one of the choice gems of which there are scores in ruins.

80. Amidst the modern vulgarities in the Court of Ruanweli, one or two interesting objects remain—notably a great octagonal pillar which is reputed to have been removed from the site occupied by the pagoda ; and an image of King Batiya Tissa, now much defaced by time. This king, on account of his extraordinary piety, is said to have been the only layman ever permitted to approach the relic chamber of the pagoda. There survives also a small stone model of the stupa. It was an 11th century custom in Burma to set up models of the pagodas.

81. The main road, that runs past Ruanweli from the Brazen Palace towards Thuparama, is the old 'Sacre Road' of ancient Anuradhapura. Beside it, a stone is pointed to as being the spot where the dying Dutthagamini lay and gazed at the great shrine he had built. What good had it profited him? and to comfort the old man, his servants read out all the good deeds of his reign. It is a pathetic story, and doubtless based on fact: but unfortunately the stone does not mark where he really lay, because it belongs to a building dating from nearly a thousand years later.

. . . . .

82. Great and interesting monuments, some of them world-famous, are these which we have grouped together as the least attractive because of the somewhat squalid character of their present surroundings. Let us now proceed deeper into the Mahamegha Garden, and see that which is unspoilt; that upon which Time has conferred a gracious beauty, and which antiquity has endowed with an atmosphere of repose. Beyond the huge brick mound of Ruanweli spread lawns, green and lush, shaded with glorious rain trees, and scattered over with groups of slender granite columns. Pillars, pillars! There are acres of them upon the grassland. Old steps, porches, bedragoned balustrades, lie about in profusion. The

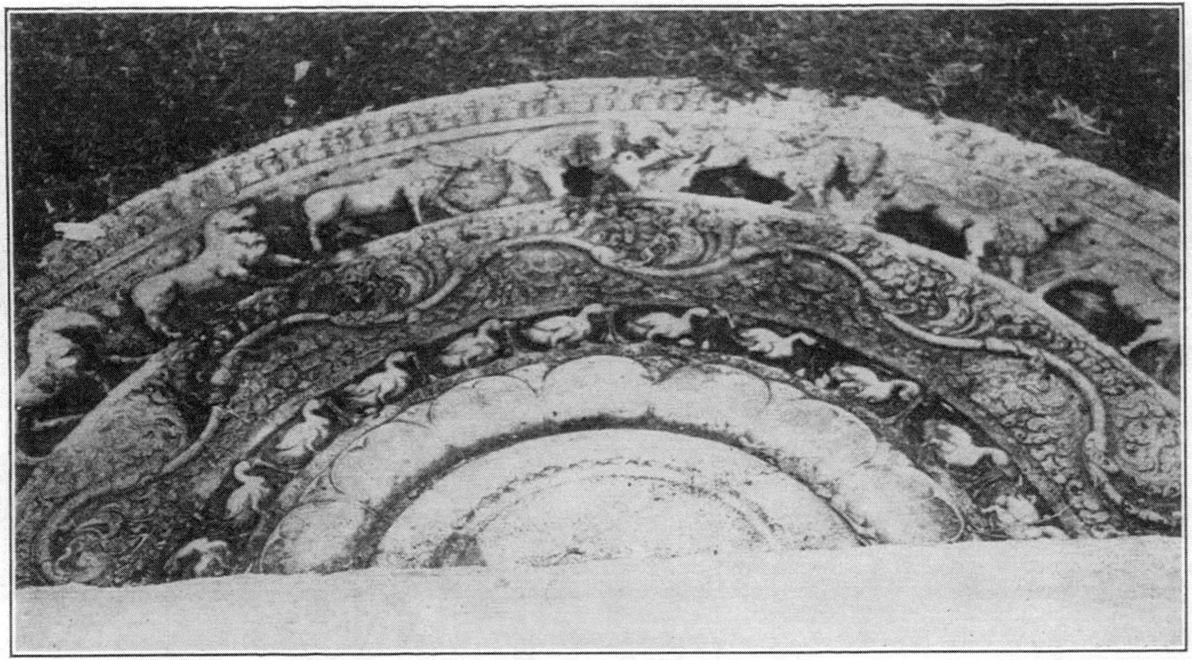

MOON STONE (ANURADHAPURA)

The bottom tread of the stairway is a carved, semicircular stone. The heart is a lotus, expanding in concentric rings into a design of geese, foliage, and animals.

*Facing page* 54

'Moon Stones' in this neighbourhood are amongst the best. Convention claims our first attention for the great historic monuments: but it is to these unconsidered gems, so charming, so appealing, that one turns with instinctive delight. This 'Moon Stone,' for instance—the semicircular bottom tread of a flight of steps—its heart is a lotus, expanding in concentric rings into a design of geese and foliage, and lastly an outer ring of elephants, bulls, horses, and lions, all life-like and spirited. The elephants are particularly animated. 'Moon Stones' are a feature of Polonnaruwa also, but there they are more laboured and crowded. Here in Anuradhapura, we see them in all the exuberance of early art. There are several pavilions and other buildings on this lawn. One of the best groups of pillars is popularly known as 'Queen's Pavilion.'

83. The stairs, of which 'Moon Stones' are the lowest step, are flanked by dragon-shaped balustrades, some with grotesque figures, or *Dwa pals*, as sentinels. In addition, there may be, perhaps, a couple of 'Guard Stones,' decorated with figures of *Naga-raja*, to keep the entrance safe from evil influences. Very often the steps lead up to a porch, of which the floor may be ten feet square. It is made of one single block of stone, weighing several tons. With sketch-book and camera, one can wander indefinitely through

King Tissa's Mahamegha Garden, noting how Time in two millenniums has torn vast monuments to pieces, but whimsically spared here or there some comparatively fragile detail.

84. In 1860 Tennent described "thick forest which covers everything with an impenetrable shade, except where the piety of pilgrims has caused a space to be cleared round the principal Monuments." Things are very different to-day. A curious and pleasing feature of nearly all these old sites of Ceylon is the park-land in which they lie. For some happy reason, jungle undergrowth now shows no inclination to spring up. Perhaps the grazing of cattle keeps it down. The Archæological Department, of course, has done a lot of clearing, but this is not sufficient to account for all the park-land which seems rather to resemble the 'Patana' or grassland of the hills, modified by lowland conditions. It is possible that long periods of intense cultivation may help the land to resist a subsequent growth of heavy jungle. Whatever the reason for their existence, these parks set off to perfection the ruins that lie scattered across them. All day shadows lie black and alluring under the trees, and in the evening the sunshine steals over the turf with that quality of repose that one associates somehow with English lawns. Many charming birds are seen amongst the ruins. The commonest are the Indian

A PORCH

Steps lead up to a porch, of which the floor may be ten feet square, and made of one single block of stone weighing many tons.

*Facing page* 56

Black-headed Oriole (*Oriolus luteolus luteolus*) ; the exquisite Paradise Fly-catcher (*Tersephone paridisi paridisi*) ; and the Black-backed Robin, which here finds plenty of stone pillars and monoliths to play about on.

84A. The question is often argued whether Anuradhapura the first capital, or Polonnaruwa the second, is the most interesting, or the most attractive. In my opinion there is no doubt about it but that Anuradhapura is superior from every point of view. Its monuments were built by giants, as compared with those at Polonnaruwa, which are the works of mere men. Anuradhapura is the expression of an exuberant culture in the vigour of youth, while Polonnaruwa is the last effort of its decay. Anuradhapura is essentially Buddhist and Sinhalese : Polonnaruwa is the work of hired foreign architects—and Hindu architects at that. Lastly, the monuments of Anuradhapura, even in their more advanced decay, are altogether grander and bigger. There is a richer variety in the capitals of their numberless pillars, and in their 'guard-stones' and balustrades—though how much of all this belongs to restorations of the Polonnaruwa period (and they were extensive under Wijaya Bahu and Prakrama) it is hard to say. The 'Moon Stones' of the first capital, at any rate, are incomparably the finest. Besides all this, Anuradhapura covers a large area of country. Its ruins, as

Knox described them in his hurried flight, are indeed a "world of hewn stone." Above all, the older capital is saturated with an antiquity, beside which Polonnaruwa is a mere mushroom. Comparisons, however, are futile. Polonnaruwa has its own charm, but it is of another kind.

. . . . .

85. There is no single monument that brings home more vividly the extreme antiquity of Anuradhapura than the Thuparama, 307 B.C. 307 B.C.!! Thuparama was contemporary with Asoka. It is the oldest building, not only in Ceylon, but in the whole of India. It has no doubt lost something of its original shape in the process of numerous restorations, but as we have already noted, the Sinhalese are conservative in the matter of architecture. The stupa in Ceylon has always remained a stupa, and has not undergone such changes as those effected by the more imaginative Burmese. Nevertheless, it is well to repeat with regard to the ancient monuments of Anuradhapura that some of them must have been restored again and again, and that we are not now in a position to estimate the effect of those renovations. Mr. Hocart has pointed out that in Ceylon brickwork developed earlier than stone. He is of opinion, however, that the original Thuparama was not of solid brick, but that it seems to have been an interesting

transition between the earth barrow and the solid brick tope.[1]

86. Thuparama, as we have seen, was built by King Tissa immediately after his conversion to Buddhism. It is reputed to contain the collar-bone of the Buddha. Tissa lived till 267 B.C., and Mahinda survived him by eight years. The pagoda is now bell-shaped, and its most interesting features are the tall, slender, pillars that surround it. These are probably a later addition. They are 26 feet high, and are arranged in four concentric rings, the pillars of the inner ring being only about two and a half feet apart. These lichen-grown shafts are mainly octagonal, but with the lower part cut squares, and they are surmounted with graceful capitals. The use to which they were originally put is rather obscure. They may have supported awnings above the pagoda court, or even some more solid form of roof. Or they may have carried streamers like the *Tagun-daing* pillars of Burma, and the ' Prayer Flag ' poles of Tibet. But in any case, the effect of this forest of dainty stone masts, though many of the outer ones are now broken, is still very impressive. Here the ghosts of two-and-twenty centuries haunt the venerable shrine—nearly half a cycle in Buddhist mythology !

87. South-east of Thuparama there are several

[1] Ceylon *Journal of Science*, Vol. I, Part II, page 44.

important buildings, one of which, the so-called Dalada Maligawa, is popularly supposed to have housed the Tooth Relic, though the late Mr. Ayrton (chiefly on the authority of Fa Hien) disagrees, and believes that the real relic shrine was a few hundred yards to the north-east of Thuparama, and inside what was once the city wall. As far as can be ascertained, the city lay somewhere to the right (east) of the road between Thuparama and Abhayagiri (Northern Stupa). Presumably the successive palaces were located there, though their identification is still uncertain. It is at any rate a fact that in later days the Tooth Relic was always kept close to the palace —as at Polonnaruwa, and finally at Kandy. If the brick building called Gedigé, or Fruit House, represents the palace, then the true Dalada Maligawa is probably one of the ruins near it. Sinhalese palaces were always a collection of comparatively small houses.

88. To the west of Thuparama is an embankment with the Basawak Kulama Lake beyond. (*Kulama* is the Tamil word for 'lake,' as *wewa* is the Sinhalese). It is reputed to have been constructed in 505 B.C., so that it is now nearly 2500 years old! That is, it belongs to that remote age of Vijaya when the Sinhalese, by developing their system of irrigation, were paving the way for glories to come. But with regard to the date, it has very probably been put back

a century or so by early chronologists in their anxiety to make Vijaya's landing coincide with the death of Buddha. The face of the embankment is lined with the most splendid rain trees I have ever seen. At the moment I climbed it, the sun was setting, and under the rain trees night was already gathering on the grassland: but on the embankment I was met with a blaze of white sunshine. The contrast between dusk and day was very striking, and gave the great trees a curiously unreal appearance. From the bright sunshine you looked back as upon some darkened stage scene. Then quickly the sun disappeared, and the wide, shining expanse of the lake, surrounded by its domes of foliage, suddenly turned grey, as night finally settled down on Anuradhapura.

89. There are three great lakes in the vicinity of the old city, each with a beauty of its own—the Basawak Kulama (505 B.C.): the Tissa Wewa (about 300 B.C.): and the Nuwara Wewa or 'City Lake' which is of a somewhat later date, probably 1st century A.D. The Tissa Wewa drains into the Basawak Kulama. In Tennent's day these lakes were mere pestiferous swamps, and they were not repaired till about 1870. Their destruction is always attributed to their having been breached by the Tamils: but it is possible that their Sinhalese creators did not

allow sufficient spill' ways, and that when neglected the lakes ultimately breached themselves.

. . . . .

90. Nearly all early writers have exaggerated the size of the monuments of Anuradhapura. But three, at least, may be justly described as 'gigantic': the Ruanweli (137 B.C.), the Abhayagiri (87 B.C.), and the Jetawana-rama (A.D. 255). All three are huge hemispherical stupas. The first, as already noted, has been partially restored. The other two are still overgrown with shrubs, and on that account have retained an air of antiquity. Fifty years ago they were covered, not with shrubs, but with great trees, which were tearing down the brickwork: and indeed the debris of fallen material at their base is five or six feet deep. But even in the case of the most decayed buildings, they have been repaired again and again during the course of centuries, and it is impossible now, even from the size of the bricks, to ascertain what is original, or to what period the restorations really belong. These stupas (with the exception of the lately restored Ruanweli) now have the appearance of shrubby hills, rising majestically out of the trees at their feet, and capped with the characteristic box-like structure, and spire or *hti*. It is hard to believe that such colossal mounds are really composed of solid brick. Yet such is the case. Bricks that I

measured at Abhayagiri were found to be 20 inches long, 10½ inches broad, and 3½ inches deep.

91. For many years there has been confusion as to which stupa is really the Abhayagiri and which the Jetawana-rama. The public has transposed the names, and the error, which has been followed by most writers, is hard to eradicate. Many of the names now in common use have been recovered from the *Mahawansa*, and it can be readily understood how easily topography may be confused when it relies on a book of that sort, or on such authorities as the Chinese traveller Fa Hien. The popular belief that the great Eastern Dagoba (that nearest Ruanweli) was the Abhayagiri was first questioned by Nevill in 1888. Messrs. Ayrton and Hocart have since proved conclusively that it is not.[1] In this book the correct names are given—Jetawana-rama to the great Eastern Stupa, and Abhayagiri to the great Northern Stupa.

92. It is important to make this troublesome departure from the already well-established nomenclature because the Abhayagiri, by reason of its connection with the 'heretical sect,' is, historically, by far the most important of the two. "There was," says Ayrton[2], "a continual struggle going on at Anura-

[1] *Archæological Survey*, Ceylon, Vol. I, 1924, page 10.

[2] Memoir. *Archæological Survey*, Vol. I, page 17

dhapura between the Maha Vihare with its orthodox attachment to the Hinayanist doctrine, and the Abhayagiri fraternity who were ready to adopt any new variation of Mahayanist Buddhism." The latter favoured corrupt and dangerous doctrines, and were frequently chastised by various kings: but in spite of this, they gained the ascendency at several periods, notably in the reign of Maha Sen, when the orthodox priests abandoned Anuradhapura for a time, and fled to Rohana. For these reasons the correct identification of the two stupas is very desirable.

93. The Jetawana-rama, or Eastern Stupa, was built by Maha Sen, the last king of the 'Great Dynasty' in the 3rd century A.D. The diameter, according to Tennent, is 360 feet, and the height 250 feet: and it is about this colossal shrine that rather misleading statistics have been given concerning imaginary towns and tunnels that could be made out of its bricks. Certainly, it is an enormous building, and without doubt represents the sweat and anguish of a generation.

94. The surrounding country is deeply shaded by rain trees, and one comes out of the shadows to be confronted quite suddenly by the towering monument. Its steps and approaches, though massive, are dwarfed by the great bulk of the pagoda. The platform on which the stupa stands is paved with granite

ABHAYAGIRI

" The stupendous dimensions, and the waste of labour, are hardly outdone by the pyramids of Egypt."

*Facing page 64*

flags, many of which have been forced from their beds by the stress of Time. There are traces of altars at the four points of the compass—some of them splendid creations of stone, backed with a design of elephants. (Better preserved examples may be seen, however, at another of the stupas called Miri-siwettye). The platform is littered with pillars, altars and 'Naga Stones' lying in confusion. A rough path climbs the now crumbling, shrub-grown dome: and from the summit there is a superb view towards Nuwara-wewa Lake and Mahintale Hill in one direction, and in the other towards the two other great topes that rise up out of the foliage of the plain. The upper brickwork, or box-like *dhatu gharba*, of the dagoba itself has been restored on three sides. It is a brick imitation of a 'Buddhist rail,' after the plan of the Sanchi Tope. Above this massive square structure, rises the *hti*, or spire, of which about half remains.

95. The Abhayagiri Stupa is almost exactly like the above, so it need not detain us long. It was built by Walagam Bahu to commemorate the expulsion of the Tamils in 87 B.C. The place is chiefly of interest because of its connection with the Mahayanist School, the heretical Dhammaruci.

96. In the neighbourhood of Abhayagiri—that is to the north and west of it—the park-land is continued,

and here we come to one of the most charming parts of Anuradhapura. Such a profusion of ruins there is! Pillars—erect, falling and prone, singly and in thick clumps, cover acres of ground. Plinths, troughs, stairs, pavilions, 'moon stones' and inscribed monoliths are scattered in wild disorder over the turf. Here sits a mutilated Buddha in solitary contemplation. There, a dainty pavilion has been re-roofed to show the former beauty of these ruins. In all directions are seen the accessories of wealth and culture, and, it is to be feared, the indolence and luxury of the indulgent Mahayanist priests from the adjacent and richly endowed Abhayagiri, whose headquarters were at the beautiful monastery of Ratna Pasada. (The term *Pasada* means palace, temple, shrine or raised platform, and is in fact identical with *Maligawa*.)

97. The Ratna Pasada, or Jewel Palace, is a ruin close to the Outer Circular Road, and is easily identified by its massive pillars, and by the exquisite beauty of its one remaining 'guard stone.' 'guard stones' are two ornamental slabs placed at the foot of a stairway, and the figure on this one is enriched with draperies, jewels and floral devices. The whole composition is in the best style—free, graceful, and perfectly finished. The site was excavated in 1912, though the 'guard stone' itself seems to have been found, at a depth of seven feet, by Burrows in 1885.

RATNA PASADA (ANURADHAPURA)

The one remaining " Guard Stone " is richly carved. It was found buried at a depth of 7 feet, and is ascribed to the eighth century.

*Facing page 66*

The sedent Buddha near by was recovered at the same time.

98. The present Ratna Pasada rests on an older building, which there is reason to believe was built by King Gaja Bahu (A.D. 171–193).[1] An inscription found there gives the full titles of the Abhayagiri Stupa—*Abhaya gamini utara maha ceta*. The present platform, and possibly the exquisite 'guard stone,' may belong to the restoration of Mahinda II, who spent 300,000 pieces of gold on the building in the 8th century A.D.[2] The monastery was subsequently robbed of much of its stone, and one huge pillar has been found "probably dropped and left to its fate" near the Kali Kovil.[3] The excavation of the Ratna Pasada, its identification, and the resetting of its shattered platform and steps, is an example of the useful work being done by the Archæological Department.

99. A word concerning 'guard stones' may not be out of place here. Like many other architectural features, they are helpful in dating the building to which they belong. 'Guard stones' seemed to have developed out of the idea of a lotus bud, and early examples curve upwards on top into a little point

[1] Memoir. *Archæological Survey*, Vol. I, 1924, page 2.
[2] Memoir. *Archæological Survey*, Vol. I, 1924, page 10.
[3] Memoir. *Archæological Survey*, Vol. I, 1924, page 5.

which, as time went on, was gradually flattened out. Such ancient 'guard stones' are often quite plain, or they are decorated with a vase, or with a grotesque dwarfish figure. The grotesque figures on the 'guard stones' at the Northern Stupa, and at the east entrance of Ruanweli, are amongst the few examples of that type still in position, though others exist in the Museum at Colombo. They are not common. With the evolution of 'guard stones,' may be noticed that of the balustrades of the stairways. These, in early examples, are quite straight, or they may be curved, though without any suggestion of the *Makara*, or dragon. As the base-decorated 'guard stone' develops mouldings at its base, so the balustrade tends to become more ornate. Pilasters are added, and the curved outline assumes the form of a dragon. The 'guard stone' in its final stage becomes quite rounded at the top, and the graceful Naga Raja figure appears on its face. This is essentially the Polonnaruwa type and its appearance at Anuradhapura (where it is quite common) denotes the restoration period of Polonnaruwa. Kings—notably Vijaya Bahu and Prakama. The single 'guard stone' at Ratna Pasada described above seems to be an exception. It appears too excellent for the decadent Polonnaruwa period and has been assigned to the 8th century.

100. Many other kinds of stones are seen lying

"GUARD STONES"

*Facing page 68*

about, of which the most curious are canoe-shaped troughs. There is one near Ratna Pasada that is 63 feet long. These troughs were used for the offerings of rice to priests, their extraordinary size, I suppose, being intended to suggest the generosity of the royal donor. It is hard to believe they were ever filled with rice : but on the other hand we have to remember that Anuradhapura was infested by thousands of hungry and politically minded priests, whom it was no doubt desirable that the King should support in comfort. The troughs are usually found on the site of Alms Houses.

101. Other curious stones seen lying about are carved with square holes, like chess boards. These were placed beneath Buddha images, and are believed to have been intended for the depositing of relics. Here and there, as at Thuparama, coffin-shaped blocks are found, with a hollow, roughly suggesting the human form. These are supposed to have been used for embalming, or some such process. (Dead monks in Burma are still preserved in honey pending a suitable time for cremation.)

102. Few people wander along this Outer Circular Road ; and the ruins bask undisturbed in the sunshine, or dream in the shadows of a splendour that is gone. Lizards skip upon the baths and couches of prince, priest, and noble. A Paradise Flycatcher, in

rich chestnut plumage, hunts from a fallen monolith. Golden orioles and turquoise kingfishers dart through the trees. Over all has fallen a leafy cloak, and the mantle of that Peace which passes understanding, when proud monuments yearn no more for the glory that is gone. They are a tale that is told. They have their legend, and rest content.

103. The Outer Circular Road loops for miles through scenes like these. Where it joins 'Y Road,' lies the supposed tomb of Dutthagamini, and close by stands the Lankarama Dagoba amidst a litter of ruin. So we return to Anuradhapura by way of the lake called Tissa. Here (close to the Jail) lies the Miri-siwettye (Dutthagamini 161 B.C.)—a vast brick hemisphere which owes its restoration to the munificence of the late King of Siam. Though dwarfed by the other great stupas, and only fourth in point of size, it is no mean building. In design, it closely resembles the others: so that their altars at the four points of the compass can be restored in imagination from those seen here, which are in better preservation. These altars are massive structures of granite, about 20 feet high, and ribbed with bars, like the rungs of a fence. Low down there is a fresco of elephants' heads, and higher up a less perfect one of horses and lions. The whole composition is massive and dignified: but we can note here how slavishly the architects were following

Facing page 70

a stereotyped design. The story goes that it was Dutthagamini's unvarying custom to share his food with the monks. (It was probably politic to do so !) Having forgotten this formality on one occasion while eating a chilli, he expiated the misdeed by building this stupa. Hence its name, from *miri*, a chilli.

104. Near by, is a collection of giant pillars popularly known as the 'Elephant Stable,' but which, like the Ratna Pasada, seems to have been one of the monasteries of the heretical Dhammaruci sect. The pillars here are large, but very rough.

105. It was at a low platform close to this monument that, immersed in my thoughts, I became suddenly entangled in a ridiculous comedy. From four directions, all unaware of the others' approach, there met on the platform a black cat, a cow, a six-foot snake and myself. For nearly a minute we all stopped dead—the snake being evidently much the most apprehensive. Suddenly, the cow took action by charging me. Pussy and I ignobly took to the trees. I don't know what happened to the snake. But the cow held the field for some time.

106. A path follows the embankment of the Tissawewa Lake, past a group of queer boulders beneath which two little baths are situated, which in former days must have been very charming. One of the rocks is carved with a circular design which some

think to be a map, but which appears to me to be an astrological formula (like the 'Yodiya' stones of Arakan) to avert evil from some particular direction.

107. Close by is the Rock Temple of Isurumuniya Vihare, which belongs to the early period of Tissa (307 B.C.). This is a very curious spot. An outcrop of large granite boulders has been built up into a temple, with a pool before it. The face of the rock is carved with figures, notably a spirited elephant with trunk raised, standing half-submerged in the pool. Another unfinished group of elephants is in a simpler style, and is evidently by another artist. The seated figure of a man is remarkable for its contemplative attitude. One arm is rested on the knee very naturally. There is a horse's head behind. Mr. Hocart thinks these sculptures are only part of some unfinished composition, dating from the 7th or 8th centuries.[1] A portrait, popularly supposed to be that of Asoka Mala (the son of Dutthagamini) and his wife, seated together in a very friendly and intimate manner, is also charming. Inside the temple there are some moulded modern figures of considerable merit.

108. An adjacent mound is pointed out as the tomb of Elala, the Tamil king slain by Dutthagamini, who chivalrously raised this monument after their personal combat. The tomb of Elala was long held in special

[1] Ceylon *Journal of Science*, Vol. I, Part III, page 96.

ISSURU-MUNIYA at ANURADHAPURA
A ROCK TEMPLE BY KING TISSA, 300 B.C., ALSO TWO
OF THE SCULPTURES FROM ITS WALLS

*Facing page 72*

reverence by the Sinhalese, but now it is a shapeless mass of rubbish. Parker questioned the correct identity of the mound, but Mr. Hocart, the present Commissioner of Archæology, supports the popular tradition, pointing out that kings were frequently buried in Dagobas.

109. One last cluster of ruins we may mention—those of Toluvila beside the railway station. The group consists of two platforms, 500 yards apart, each on a high mound, and joined by a stone causeway. The whole site is admirably planned, and when originally the two monuments faced each other with the causeway between, they must have been very beautiful. The 'guard stones' are plain, and of archaic type. The ruin, concerning which nothing is known, may be about 9th century.

110. It is difficult at this advanced stage in the restoration of Anuradhapura to appreciate the achievement of the Archæological Department. It has been truly said of the East that the Archæologist is the friend of the people—and here it should be more than ever true. Science has delivered cities from oblivion, arrested their decay, and restored them to history as the proof of past splendours in which we could not otherwise believe. Centuries ago, the Tamil 'let in the jungle' upon Anuradhapura. Now the site is being retrieved. No longer do roots tug at the

brickwork—at least in the principal monuments. After so many vicissitudes, the grey and ancient stones take their rest upon the turf-land. But their secret is not yet fully declared. Excavation, particularly at minor sites, will throw light upon the habits of those long-forgotten generations, and will show us how, in the early centuries of our era, people lived in Ceylon, and who they were. Scientific investigation is urgently needed ; for the Present with all its complex problems is rooted in the Past. What we need to find now in ancient Anuradhapura are not any more spectacular monuments, but some good, sordid, rubbish heaps.

## CHAPTER VI

## SIGIRIYA

### The Zenith and Decline

111. To preserve our chronological order, we must now turn to sites lying at the feet of the Kandyan Hills.

112. Matale is the "Maha Talawa" of the *Mahawansa*, and in its historic capacity it holds a unique place in literature as the site at which the Buddhist legend was committed to writing in the 1st century B.C., after being handed down orally for four hundred years. It belongs to that remote age when, before the beginning of the Christian era, Ceylon had already evolved her remarkable culture. But, as we have seen, even those were troubled times: and King Walagam Bahu, having been deposed by Tamil invaders, wandered about the southern mountains for fifteen years. On his restoration, he converted into temples some of the caves in which he had sought refuge. The greatest of these is at Dambulla. Another one, called Alu-wihara, is here at Matale: and it was in this shrine that, later on, the Buddhist Scriptures were written down by order of the King.

113. Alu-wihara lies two miles to the north of

Matale, at the foot of a green and mist-swept mountain. Some vast masses of granulite have been thrown together, and amidst these are various caves embellished with paintings and statues of the Buddha. Upon a high rock is perched a little white pagoda, and from here you look down among the boulders, as into a chasm. It is a very extraordinary place: for the gaunt and precipitous rocks are now embowered in trees, and approached by a flight of stone steps. The picturesque appearance of Alu-wihara is, however, the least of its attractions. Its real interest lies in the work that was here completed—the preservation of the *Tri Pittaka*, the "Three Baskets of the Law," for the comfort and guidance of Gods and Men. It can easily be imagined that the place is as interesting to Buddhists, as would be the site at which the Bible was written—did such a site exist.

114. One of the caves is dedicated to the learned Buddha Ghosa, who retranslated the Sinhalese text into Pali, and so gave the Buddhist Scriptures the fixed form they have since retained. According to a popular legend, it was he who introduced Buddhism into Burma. For this reason, also, Alu-wihara is a favourite resort of Burmese pilgrims, whose names are written on the walls of this cave. The Burmese, alas! have an irresistible craving for scrawling on monuments.

'Alu Wihara'.
At this place the Buddhist Scriptures were written down
in the 1st Century B.C. after being handed on orally for four hundred years.

*Facing page 76*

115. Only a student of Buddhism can realize the flood of literature that for two millenniums has resulted from Walagam Bahu's 'good deed.'

116. The drive of 28 miles to Dambulla is a pretty one. The elevation of the plain is only 500 feet, and in April the climate is hot, though not oppressive. The nights at least are cool. There are many rubber plantations by the roadside, and cocoa is grown all the way to Nalanda, the half-way stage. At Nalanda there is an important ruin of a temple called Gedigé, dating from the 7th century. It is said to be in the Palava style, but, unfortunately, I was unaware of its existence, and did not see it.

117. Beyond Nalanda a radical change takes place in the aspect of the country. Widespread cultivation ceases; and, as we descend definitely to the plains, jungle commences. For, just as the now highly productive mountains to the south of the Island were formerly waste land, considered by the ancient Sinhalese as uninhabitable except for outlaws and refugees, so the areas that they made to flower as a garden have now relapsed into mosquito-ridden forest. Over ancient Sinhala has spread an impenetrable undergrowth.

118. The road gradually descends to these wooded plains, though outlying spurs of the Kandyan Hills are still strung across the lowlands either in the form

of picturesque ranges, or as isolated bosses of granulite. Several kinds of dry-zone trees make their appearance —cactus, acacia, and neem.

. . . . .

119. Dambulla is celebrated for its Cave Temples. These consist of three chambers high up on a granite hill. The central one is perhaps sixty yards long, and thirty broad. Probably the cave is partly natural, but it has evidently been hewn out and finished off in places. It now possesses a hideous façade of modern porches. The roof of the cavern is painted, and slopes back, and the rear wall is about twelve feet high. The sides are lined with figures of Buddha, some of which are cut out of the solid rock. A small pagoda rises from the floor of the cave: and one or two inappropriate Hindu Deities are included amongst the Buddhist images. The most interesting figure, however, is that of King Walagam Bahu who, as a fugitive, sought refuge in this cave, and afterwards converted it into a temple. His statue, which represents him as rather a portly person, is about ten feet high. Another large wooden figure depicts King Kirti Nissanka who restored the temple in the 12th century, after it had been spoiled by Tamil invaders. The only real interest of this cave is its association with these princes, and its great antiquity as a place of pilgrimage. It dates from the 1st century B.C. But

otherwise it has little to recommend it. It entirely lacks the grandeur of the limestone caves of Burma, whose Buddhas and Pagodas are placed in a natural and romantic setting.

120. But the approach to the Dambulla Caves, and the hill in which they are situated, are altogether more attractive than the temple itself. The hill is about 500 feet high, the caves being situated near the top. The ascent is first over long slopes of naked granulite, and then up picturesque stairs, which pick their way between huge boulders. In places, these steps are well shaded. In the distance can be seen the bold and solitary rock-fortress of Sigiriya. From the piazza of the temple you look down over cactus, peepul, and flowering champac, to the multi-coloured foliage of the plain, and beyond that again to the bold and beautiful mountains of Kandy. It is truly a wide and lovely view, in which the dingy cave is but an incident.

121. The reverse side of the hill also, is very curious. The black granulite is entirely exposed and treeless, and has assumed a smooth surface and a rounded outline, so that, as seen from the Rest House, it has the appearance of a gigantic hemisphere. There does not appear to be a single crack or cleft, and the whole mountain is in fact one colossal boulder. This formation is characteristic of Ceylon. Many other

hills, particularly in the neighbourhood of Maho, Yapahuwa, and Kurunegala are smooth, flawless stones.

122. The *fauna* of these low, forested plains is altogether more interesting than that of the over-cultivated mountains. Wild elephants are numerous. They still resort at night to many jungle roads in Ceylon, and this is true even of the better populated areas in the south of the Island, as between Wellawaya and the coast, where it is not safe to travel after dark. Elephants are sometimes very destructive: but even so, there seems little justification for the slaughter boasted of in Forbes' *Ceylon*. He mentions in one place 9 elephants shot before breakfast, and in another 106 killed in three days. The shooting of elephants is now prohibited, except in the case of 'proscribed' rogues. Their numbers are increasing: but comparatively few males have good tusks.

123. The only other really dangerous animal is the bear which is apt to attack at sight, and has an evil reputation. The tiger does not occur, but the cats are represented by a leopard, and a very magnificent Fishing Cat.

124. Of course there are many deadly snakes, notably the cobra and the Tik-palonga, which I believe is the Russel's Viper. The Hamadryad is unknown. Snakes are generally said to be rarely

ELEPHANTS

Their numbers are increasing, but comparatively few males have good tusks.

*Facing page* 80

seen except after rain, when they are tempted to seek shelter in houses. This was not my experience. Perhaps I was out in the jungle more than is usual : but at any rate I saw snakes daily. Unlike those of the Malay Peninsula, which are largely arboreal, the majority keep to the ground in Ceylon. Two large snakes were standing up to each other entwined under the great tree in the Rest house garden at Dambulla : and in the Post Office a swarm of very tiny bees was attempting to hive in the letter-box.

125. On the hill there are fine tortoises with whitish lines and stars on their shells. After rain, tortoises are seen literally in scores in wayside puddles. At Polonnaruwa I shared my bedroom for a week with a most entertaining little tree-frog, which was able to jump on to any vertical surface and adhere to it by means of little suckers on its toes. In this low country, too, I frequently saw a curious mongoose with a bushy tail. A very large and handsome squirrel occurs in these forests, which is evidently allied to *Ratufa malabarica*, and to the 'Malay Pied Giant Squirrel.'[1] The underparts are whitish, the back grey and reddish, shading to fawn on the tail. The top of the head, and the two fore-paws, are black.

126. Birds are very numerous. The Iora, and the lovely green Bee-eater make their appearance : and

[1] Enriquez' *Malaya*, pages 72 and 260.

the brilliant plumage of Roller and Kingfisher are seen in the foliage. The beautiful song of the Indian Shama (*Kittocincla macroura indica*) is constantly heard. All day there is a calling and a whistling: and after dark the nightjars begin to cast stones over ice.

. . . . .

127. From Dambulla to Sigiriya is eleven miles by road—eleven miles of glorious jungle. Sigiriya Rock, as we have seen, is a monument to the decline of ancient Ceylon. Five hundred years have passed since Walagam Bahu founded Dambulla. The first great Dynasty has given way to kings whose ceaseless and monotonous feuds have reduced the Sinhalese to ruin.

128. In the middle of the 5th century, Prince Kassiyappa, having walled up alive his father Dhatu Sen (he who ordered the *Mahawansa* to be written) ascended the throne: and in the face of his sullen and resentful people, retired to the rock-pinnacle of Sigiriya whence he ruled for eighteen years (from A.D. 459), till defeated and killed by his brother. The incident is told with much feeling by the author of the *Mahawansa* who was himself the uncle of Dhatu Sen, a witness of his horrible death, and the comforter of his last hours. In truth there is little to be said in favour of Kassiyappa, except that they were

rough days in which he lived. In Sinhalese history he is the villain of the play.

129. The strategic value of Sigiriya is obvious. Facing north, the parricide King had his capital and his subjects before him at his mercy. Behind lay the trackless and then uninhabited mountains of Kandy. Sigiriya itself—the Lion Rock—was a castle, unapproachable, impregnable.

130. From the plain it rises straight into the air to a height of about 400 feet, embattled on every side with sheer precipices. Indeed, where the cliffs are not perpendicular, they actually overhang. Natural fortresses of this sort are not uncommon in India, and have been similarly used by bandit-chiefs: but Sigiriya is the only one in Ceylon which has been so used, though there are many others—notably the rock at Yapahuwa—which could be easily defended. Sigiriya might be held even to-day against modern artillery.

131. Across the face of these cliffs a broad gallery was built, part of which still remains, and has been put into good repair by the Archæological Department. It is hardly possible that all the buildings at Sigiriya could have been erected within the short period of Kassiyappa's residence. No doubt the place was retained as a fortress after his time. The occurrence of lime cement in portions of the gallery makes it

certain that that work was repaired at a later date. But for centuries the summit, where various ruins and baths survive, was unapproachable, except to a few expert climbers. The rock is now safely scaled by iron stairs and galleries, though they are sufficiently giddy to deter anyone with a bad head. The area at the summit is about one acre in extent. In certain crevices of the rock there are painted frescoes. They can only be approached by rope ladders, but copies of the frescoes can be seen in the Museum at Colombo, and with these most people content themselves.

132. The view from Sigiriya Rock, especially in the evening, is perfectly magnificent. The forests of the plain, where already night is creeping, are rich with every hue of deep green, shading to blue where the distant hills of Kandy lie along the horizon. Frequent swamps—the wreck of former irrigation works—catch the glimmer of the fading light. Thousands of swallows hurl themselves into the abyss from the granulite wall of Sigiriya, or surge up to it again in twittering waves. The sunset sky is pale green, suffused with salmon-pink : and with a few rich purple clouds riding into the dying day. And as you return slowly home in the dusk, rays of saffron light shoot up out of the West, and bathe the grim rock-walls in one last radiant glow.

133. The surroundings of Sigiriya are quite ideal.

## CHAPTER VI

There is a comfortable Rest House with snipe shooting at the very door. The country round about is littered with large boulders scattered about on turf, and shaded by trees whose shadows are black and inviting. Sigiriya is a place to stay at and enjoy for several days, and those who hurry away after merely climbing the rock miss a great deal. From the foot of the ascent a shaded path runs for a long way through woods, and affords several unusual glimpses of the fortress. It was here that the old town was situated. It was surrounded by a rampart ; and the remains of tanks and steps are still visible. The population of the 5th century was considerable, and the people were made to work. Vast masses of squared stone lie derelict in the forest, built up into cyclopean walls whose use it is now difficult to guess. King Kassiyappa, his wives, and a few trusted friends alone occupied the palace at the summit of the rock. The galleries were held by picked guards, and neither the people nor the soldiers were permitted to approach their guilty and suspicious prince. Kassiyappa did all that a Buddhist King could do to wipe out the memory and demerit of his crime, but the people never forgot or forgave ; for the father (Dhatu Sen) who had been so cruelly murdered (he was walled up alive as we have seen) had freed the country of the Malabaris, and was much beloved.

134. Even close behind the Rest House, there are some delightful rambles. Here again, the boulders are piled up in wild confusion, and you come out quite unexpectedly on to the brow of a cliff which commands a lovely view of the Kandyan hills. This is the resort of many fine butterflies. They seem to delight in hurling themselves over the abyss into the tree-tops below.

135. At the foot of the Great Rock, there is a large tank, or lake, upon whose surface is mirrored the natural fort. The outline from this direction is more than usually eccentric. Originally the rock was surrounded by a moat, the lake forming part of that system.

136. Into the cool waters of the tank, buffaloes sink of an evening, contentedly groaning. A brilliant kingfisher takes post on a tree, and a snow-white heron casts an immaculate reflection below him on the water. Long flights of steps climb laboriously to where the ancient galleries begin. And from the turf-land and the shadows, naked, sinister, domineering, rises the " Lion Hill."

## CHAPTER VII

### POLONNARUWA

### The Second Great Capital

137. Polonnaruwa was the second Sinhalese capital, which arose after the decay of the *Mahawansa*, or Great Dynasty, when the ancient city of Anuradhapura had passed finally into the hands of Tamil invaders. According to Mr. Bell, the name is of "doubtful Elu origin," and nobody seems to know what it is supposed to mean. The classical name used in the *Mahawansa* is 'Pulastipura.'

138. The site, though chosen as a place of royal residence from an early date, did not become the seat of Government till the 8th century. Tennent says: "Siri Sangabo III, without altogether deserting the old capital, made Polonnaruwa his favourite residence, and died there in A.D. 718. It had similar attractions for his successors, and Mahinda I, towards the close of the 8th century, abandoned Anarajapura. Owing to the increasing power of the Malabars, the seat of government was never permanently restored to the north. Polonnaruwa itself was captured and sacked by those insatiable marauders in 1023, and remained in their hands till recovered by Wijayo Bahu I in A.D. 1071."

139. With Wijayo Bahu, Sinhalese culture entered upon one last spurt of achievement which culminated with the national hero Prakrama Bahu, who was crowned at Polonnaruwa in A.D. 1153. It is essentially with him that the ruins are associated, and probably none of an older date survive.

140. Certain figures, even in the dark ages of history, appeal irresistibly to one's imagination, and Prakrama is one of them. He began to reign (A.D. 1153) just forty-one years after the death of another very human and lovable prince—Kyanzittha of Burma, who died in A.D. 1112. There is a curious parallel between the two. Kyanzittha rounded off the monuments of Păgān begun by his predecessors: Prakrama rounded off those of Polonnaruwa. Under these almost contemporary princes, the capitals of Burma and Ceylon achieved an extraordinary culture, till the fame of their pagodas and palaces went forth throughout all the world. Both these Kings were ardent Buddhists, and the patrons of art. Both are represented by surviving statues—that of Kyanzittha being the earliest example of portraiture in Burma: and both statues represent these successful soldiers engaged in peaceful pursuits. Kyanzittha is shown in the incomparable Ananda Pagoda that he built, kneeling in the attitude of prayer. Prakrama is represented standing, reading from a scroll.

141. Doubts have been cast by some writers on the identity of this statue, but I think we may safely accept the tradition that it does indeed represent Prakrama. Even supposing it to be the figure of a hermit, it might still represent Prakrama in a conventional ascetic guise. But as a matter of fact, if the statue was that of some 'guru,' there would certainly be symbols by which it might be recognized as such. But there are none. On the contrary, the figure is that of a bearded, corpulent man. The girdle and draperies, though worn by age, are rich. The round head-dress is not unlike the 'crown' worn by the almost contemporary statue of Kyanzittha in Burma. The image is of kingly size, and is very obviously a faithful portrait. All these are grounds for crediting the tradition that the figure is that of Prakrama. I can see no reason to doubt it.

142. The statue is approached along the embankment of the beautiful lake that Prakrama enlarged. It is about ten feet high, and is hewn out of a solitary granite boulder. The eyes are bent upon the palm-leaf book which is held in both the hands. The lower part of the body is finely draped, and is clasped at the waist by a belt. The belly is skilfully carved to give a suggestion of stoutness. The beard is full, the moustaches heavy and drooping—the general effect recalling some one of the more benevolent

Chinese gods. And there stands the King, aloof and grand, in the forest that overwhelmed the city he built. No vandal has molested his vigil: but centuries of storm have worn down the details of his features and of his dress. And as he, and his legend, and the works that he did, faded from the memory of man, we can imagine that villagers, awed by his lonely and majestic figure, invested him with divine attributes, and worshipped him as a God. Certain it is, that to this day offerings, and the grease of many candles, testify to the respect with which he is still regarded.

143. Polonnaruwa lies along the shores of Prakrama's beautiful lake—or at least did so originally. The lake, though still a large body of water, has shrunk considerably in size. It is contained by a high embankment, and on this the modern Rest House is situated. It overlooks the calm sheet of water, beyond which a chain of bold peaks is seen in the distance. At midday the white clouds that pile up over the mountains are reflected upon the placid surface of the tank. In the Topa-wewa lake you can drop into a hole among the weeds, lay down the rod, and wait for a Tank Fish to catch itself. Then you fry him and eat him: and, if the water is high and not muddy, he is excellent. But to do all this you must wade. One evening, resting from archæology,

we indulged in this mild sport. Imagine my horror an hour later, when I watched through my glasses a ten-foot crocodile enter that very patch of weeds. The sunset effects across the lake are superb. White heron wade in the shallows: and at dusk night-jars flit ghost-like along the shore. Their plaintive call is heard in the night, and also that of the cuckoo which in Burma is called '*Yauk-hpa Kwe-kaw.*' And when darkness has fallen, the fire-flies shine as I have never seen them shine elsewhere. They scintillate simultaneously, so that the foliage of the trees is continually irradiated with waves of light.

144. The original city having occupied an area of several square miles, its ruins are scattered; but they fall into several convenient groups. The first of these includes the palace and a number of temples. The palace probably dates only from the 13th century, the original one built by Prakrama having been identified by Tennent near the Jetawana-rama group. Evidently, the present building is much reduced in size since Tennent visited it. He speaks of it as being partly roofed, but it was then in the grip of fig-trees. These have since been removed. The now roofless building is of brick, its massive walls being nine feet thick. Close by is a pavilion, of which the noble stone plinth is ornamented with frescoes of lions and elephants. Dragons—or rather that mythical beast

known to Archæology as *Makara*—form the balustrades of the steps. They are so employed in Burma to this day, though in conventionalized form. This high plinth, with its ornamental stairs, was evidently a garden pleasance, or audience hall. Rows of pillars still exist which originally supported a roof. The whole palace area was enclosed with a wall, of which fragments survive here and there. The space within is a park, its turf being shaded with the foliage of many old and gracious trees. This park-like appearance, which is due to the entire absence of undergrowth, is, as already noted, a feature of all the capitals where, no doubt, trees were systematically planted in former days. Here, grey, black-faced monkeys canter over the lawns, with their long tails held straight up in the air.

145. Close to the palace is the ruin of what must once have been an exquisite bath, the Kumara Pokuna, or Prince's Bath. The floor is paved, and once steps led down into the water. The bath was originally fed by streams that flowed into it out of the mouths of stone crocodiles. Now the monoliths and lion pillars are flung about in strange confusion. But they are all there : and one has no difficulty in imagining the beauty of the scene as it must once have been when awnings were spread, and when lovely women laughed and splashed in the cool water. But now only the

A PRINCE'S BATH (POLONNARUWA)

It is not difficult to imagine the beauty of this bath when awnings were spread, and when beautiful women laughed and splashed in the cool water.

*Facing page 92*

stupid buffalo gazes upon it all with stolid indifference.

146. The temples of this group lie just outside the palace wall. Taking them in the order in which they are approached from the direction of the palace, the first is the Siva Devale I, known also as the Dalada Maligawa. Here the famous 'Tooth Relic' was housed, at least for a time. It should be remembered that originally these shrines stood on the bank of the lake, which must have greatly enhanced their beauty. Now the lake is half a mile away. Many of these monuments are surprisingly small, and this one is the smallest of them all. But it is a gem, the more fascinating on account of its smallness: for it was built with a solidity, and a regard for detail, worthy of the sacred object which for a time it housed. The walls are constructed of massive granulite blocks, once exquisitely fitted, though jungle roots have displaced many of the stones. The decorations are simple and effective. A very similar temple, called Siva Devale II, lies about half a mile distant. It has been beautifully restored, and reminded me instantly of the Temple of Pandretan in Kashmir. We may here note, once and for all, the strong Hindu influence that is visible in nearly all the monuments at Polonnaruwa. The lingam, the bull, and other Hindu symbols, as well as Hindu deities, are found everywhere.

147. The next temple of this group is a 12th-century building called Thuparama. It is made of brick, and we may note how excellent was the cement used by the ancient Sinhalese. True lime mortar was not introduced into Ceylon till the 10th century. Here, again, are seen walls of great thickness.

148. The next shrine, the Nissanka-lata-mandapaya, or 'Flower Altar of Nissanka,' is one of the artistic treasures of Polonnaruwa. It is surrounded by a modified 'Buddhist Rail,' now restored. This railing, suggestive of those at Sanchi and other Indian sites, is just like a three-runged fence, if one can imagine such a thing made of solid granite bars. The effect is very impressive. The ground-plan of the fence is rectangular, and inside it is a plinth upon which stand eight pillars. They are not straight, but bent most elegantly to resemble tree-trunks, and the theme of the lotus flower runs through the general design. The stems are draped with foliage, but the roof which once they supported has disappeared. Here, everything is of solid granite.

149. In the next shrine, the Ata-dagé, or 'House of Eight Relics,' the walls are faced with stone, but the core is of brick. The structure is chiefly remarkable for the extraordinary irregularity of the blocks of which it is built, and which are fitted and pieced together most ingeniously.

Polonnaruwa

The Kiri or 'Milk Pagoda'
So called from its original whiteness

Siva Devale II
A purely Hindu Shrine

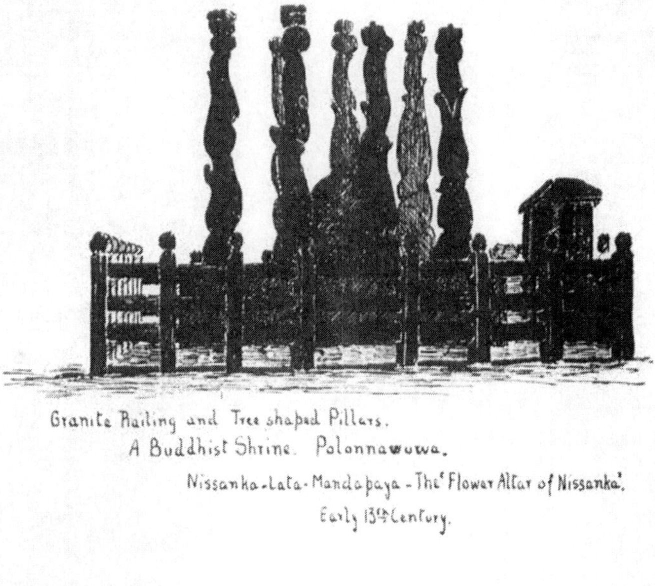

Granite Railing and Tree shaped Pillars.
A Buddhist Shrine. Polonnawuwa.
Nissanka-Lata-Mandapaya - The 'Flower Altar of Nissanka'.
Early 13th Century.

Facing page 94

150. Interest in the Sat-mahal Pasada is mainly centred upon a vast block of granulite called the Galpota, or 'Stone Book,' from its resemblance in shape to a palm-leaf manuscript. Tennent says it is 26 feet long, and 4 feet broad: and according to him, the writing with which it is inscribed says that "This engraved stone is one which the strong men of King Nissanka brought from the mountains of Mahintala and Anarajapura." Tennent points out that the distance is more than eighty miles. How the 'strong men of King Nissanka' must have hated that stone by the time they had done with it! Such were the misdirected objects upon which the energy of the nation were wasted.

151. Nissanka, or Nissanka Mala, had a passion for inscriptions. Of the fifty that survive at Polonnaruwa about three-fifths are by him, and he is even accused of putting them on the monuments of his predecessors. In spite of this wealth of inscriptions, both here and at Anuradhapura, they are of little value to chronologists, because they are usually detached from the buildings to which they refer. The Jetawanarama is a notable exception. Here an inscription has been placed on one of the 'guard stones.'

152. The last, and largest building of this group, is the Wata-dagé, or 'Circular Relic House,' a curious round brick shell, with walls now some 20 feet

high. Outside this wall, at a distance of only a couple of feet, is a low stone balustrade with floral decorations, and divided into sections by tall and graceful pillars. Round about is a court or promenade, with stairways at each of the four points of the compass. The stairs are embellished with 'Moon Stones,' of which one is a particularly fine example. The 'Moon Stones' of Polonnaruwa are less excellent than those of the first capital. They display indeed a marked decadence. Nevertheless, they are remarkable. Much care and skill was devoted to them; and for all their decadence, many are exquisitely carved and finished, so that they lend a peculiar grace and dignity to the stairways which they adorn.

. . . . .

153. The second group of ruins is a mile distant, and is reached by a path running through charming woods. It consists of the Rankot Dagoba by Nissanka (13th century), a brick hemisphere of no special interest; and the Jetawana-rama.

154. The Jetawana-rama, or to give it its correct classical name, the Lankātilaka, is one of the most important brick monuments of King Prakrama, as well as the one whose massive walls have best withstood the assault of the centuries, though there is reason to believe that the original building had fallen into ruins within a century. The inscription of the 'guard

The Jetawana-rama at Polonnaruwa. 12th Century A.D
one of the important works of King Prakrama.

Facing page 96

stone,' to which reference has already been made, records a restoration by Vijaya Bahu III in the 13th century. The popular name of Jetawana-rama, by which this pagoda is now known, seems to be a generic term for 'monastery.' The building consists of an entrance, a passage, and finally a cell for the image. The walls are still forty feet high, though the exterior decorations have mostly disappeared. Here, and elsewhere throughout the ruins, the windows are about 6½ feet high, but only 18 inches broad. The open space is divided lengthwise by a single, slender granite column. The effect is simple and elegant, if not very serviceable.

155. The entrance to the Jetawana-rama is flanked with columns, which once supported an arch, of which a fragment remains. The architecture is most unusual for a Buddhist shrine. Against the back wall of the inner 'cell' stands a colossal Buddha, now headless. To judge from the illustration in Tennent's *Ceylon* (Vol. II, page 593) this figure, in his day, was buried in rubbish up to the knees, probably with the débris of the fallen roof. It is indeed interesting to compare Tennent's accurate sketches with the monuments as they stand now. There have been great changes in seventy years. As already noted, the palace, then overgrown by trees, has been much reduced. To-day the principal buildings have been

entirely cleared of jungle. The Jetawana-rama was thoroughly excavated in 1910. Throughout these sites the brickwork has been pointed, the broken stones have been assembled, and in some places restored to their original situations. Everywhere there are signs of the expensive and affectionate care lavished upon this ancient Sinhalese capital by the British Government. It would be easier to realize this if guide-books were prepared. There is an urgent need for them. Unless a student has carefully prepared himself for his visit, he must wander blindly amongst the monuments.

156. The Jetawana-rama is so foreign to the architecture of Buddhist Ceylon that we may safely accept the statement of the *Mahawansa* that its builders were brought over from India. In the wars and invasions that preceded the period which we are considering, the arts and crafts of the Sinhalese had suffered seriously. The strong Hindu influence present in the monuments, suggest that Indian sculptors and architects were largely employed ; just as the contemporary Burmese capital of Păgān was the product of Talaing imagination fired by ideas derived in turn by them from India through Ceylon. It was an age of revivals. In England they were building Winchester Cathedral in 1079. But, whereas Păgān expressed the rising power of the Burmese, Polonnaruwa was the last effort of the decaying Sinhalese.

JETAWANA-RAMA (LEFT)

This temple is one of the most important brick monuments of King Prakrama (13th century). The building on the right is the Kiri Pagoda. (Polonnaruwa.)

*Facing page 98*

157. In Ceylon at that period, Buddhism, in this its ancient home, had lately been in danger of extinction. Wijayo Bahu (A.D. 1071), after expelling the Malabaris, had had to apply to Arakan for priests to administer the religion. Now Buddhism was restored: but it never recovered its first dominion over the imagination of the people: and that same apathy is apparent to-day.

158. Close beside the Jetawana-rama, is a large hemispherical Dagoba, the Kiri, or 'Milk Pagoda,' so called from the original whiteness of its cement facing. It dates from 1187, but is still in a good state of preservation. A group of pillars on an adjacent plinth are the remains of an ancient Council Hall.

159. To the former growth of forest trees over the *topes*, may be due the extravagant estimates that were made of the size of these remains by early writers. The ruins of Polonnaruwa are not, in fact, of any extraordinary size. In cubic content, the material of the whole lot put together would not exceed that of any single Burmese monument such as the Mingun or Dhammayan Gyi Pagodas. But in solidity, and in the excellence of workmanship, the Sinhalese buildings are much superior to many of those vast and hurried piles of shoddy that litter the banks of the Irrawaddy. On the other hand, no Sinhalese Dagoba compares with the highest Burmese Art, as

expressed by the incomparable Ananda and Gawdaw Palin Pagodas.

160. There are numerous architectural devices displayed in Polonnaruwa which suggest intimacy between Ceylon and Pågān. The most noticeable is the half-arch (the arch of which one side is cut short). It is a feature common to the Jetawana-rama of Ceylon and the Ananda of Burma. Tennent suspects that the great image in the Jetawana-rama was illuminated by a halo of light from the roof. The image in the Ananda is lit just in that way. The two buildings are of about the same date, the Ananda being the older by only 73 years.

161. The whole countryside of Polonnaruwa is a litter of ruins. There are still standing acres of those slim granite monoliths—so typical of ancient Sinhalese sites—which were used as columns for supporting roofs, or for raising buildings from the ground. The vanished superstructures were of wood, and the Tooth Temple at Kandy is a survival of this type of architecture. These slim pillars, scattered over the country, or standing derelict in groups, represent the toil of a nation. The lavish and thoughtless expenditure of labour is incredible, and could only have been indulged in by the autocratic masters of a large population.

• • • • •

162. All these monuments have their own special

ANANDA

Twelfth-century rock figures at Polonnaruwa. The " Beloved Disciple " is represented mourning beside the deceased Buddha.

*Facing page* 100

appeal, either by reason of their grace, or their historical association : but in the archæological sense the ' Black Rock Temple ' of Gal-wihara (or Kalugal-wihara, to give it its correct name) is probably the most important. Here, three colossal figures are cut from a granite wall. The seated and reclining ones are of the Buddha : the standing one, which is of very special beauty, represents Ananda, the favourite disciple, watching grief-stricken beside the reclining body of the Great Teacher, whose spirit has just entered into the bliss of Nirvana. When Lieut. Fagan discovered these monuments in 1820, he came suddenly upon this figure of Ananda, gazing at him from out of the foliage. "I cannot describe what I felt at that moment," he wrote.

163. The Ananda statue is seen to best advantage sideface, the dejected droop of the figure suggesting very poignantly the pain of parting. The features, though sorrowful, are calm. The hands are folded across the breast. The mould of the limbs is beautifully portrayed beneath the draperies. Like so many other statues at Polonnaruwa, the body is in a relaxed and natural pose—an effect obtained by swaying the hips and drooping one shoulder. This gracious Ananda, standing out like some Egyptian Prince from the wall of dark and weathered granulite is, in my opinion, a remarkable work.

164. The seated Buddha is of no artistic merit: but the 'gate' behind it represents a 'rail' with dragon-headed terminals. Its Indian origin is indicated by the copulas and other details of the background. The chief interest of the reclining Buddha is its size. It is forty-six feet in length.

165. The Gal-wihara Cave in the same rock contains a small seated Buddha which, together with its throne, is hewn out of the stone like the larger figures already described. Its features just miss perfection, but the minor decorations, and the chaste filigree work of the throne, are admirable. On each side there are attendants, or *Buddhisats*, most delicately draped and featured, and also rampant lions: and behind the central Buddha there are multi-armed figures in attitudes of adoration. Over all is placed an 'umbrella' of simple design. The whole composition is in the best Græco-Buddhist style.

166. The Gal-wihara monuments which are minutely described in the *Mahawansa*, date from the period of Prakrama at the close of the 12th century. Originally, the figures were roofed over, and the cave is but part of a monastic building that stood before it: but the Great Buddhas, and the sorrowing disciple, standing as they do against the aged and blackened rock, need no other canopy than the wide vault of heaven.

167. Tennent has called attention to the resemblance of the Gal-wihara Cave to those of Ajunta and Ellora, though its size is less ambitious. It is, in fact, quite shallow. The entrance is supported by square columns whose capitals are decorated with figures of goblins in attitudes suggesting that, like Atlas, they are upholding some great weight—in this case the roof. The idea, of course, is of Greek origin, and has spread to many countries including Burma. The Gandhara inspiration is obvious enough at Polonnaruwa ; and the beautifully draped 'attendants' mentioned above as flanking the throne of the small Buddha, may be quoted as examples of that influence. The very cave itself, cut vertically into a sloping face of rock, and carved with a long inscription, has a curiously Egyptian appearance : while the rampant lions here, as also those at the Kumara Pokuna Bath near the palace and the great lion-throne of Nissanka, are all strangely Assyrian in flavour.

. . . . .

168. A couple of miles away is the Demala Maha Saya Dagoba, or 'Northern Temple,' which resembles the Jetawana-rama on a small scale. Here, again, grotesque weight-bearing goblins occur as a frieze. Inside, there is another colossal Buddha and some crude *Jataka* frescoes. The name commonly applied to this shrine really belonged to a vast but vanished

stupa. It is now so overgrown that, though I chanced to climb it, I mistook it for a hill : and I believe that at one time its summit was the resort of wild elephants. The Lotus Bath was recently found in the adjacent jungle.

169. The floor of the Lotus Bath is a circle, scalloped to represent the eight petals of a blossom. Each of the succeeding and receding tiers of steps repeats this design, till the whole lovely lotus is complete. Mr. Mitton calls it, "A flower petrified." One can imagine how fascinating this bath must have been in those centuries of long ago, when it ran over with cool and delicious water. I can almost see the awning still, and the forms of fair women and happy children ; but it is only a vision. They are gone ! They are forgotten ! They are dust ! And the cruel jungle has torn to pieces their charming lotus flower.

. . . . .

170. On the banks of the Topa-wewa Lake, Prakrama built his Pleasure Garden, and here, close behind the Rest House, there are one or two interesting ruins which were the Audience and Council Halls of King Nissanka Malla (A.D. 1198). Only the plinths remain, and most of the massive pillars have been cast down. Here in 1820, was found the enormous 'Lion of Polonnaruwa' which is thought to have been part

of Nissanka's throne. Fifty years later it was removed to the Museum at Colombo, and its journey by road and rail is an epic. On what is not a promontory is the wreck of Prakrama's 'Island Pleasance,' which was surrounded by water when the lake stood at a higher level. This pavilion, which is extravagantly praised in the *Mahawansa*, must indeed have been a cool and delightful summer-house.

. . . . .

171. Within thirty years of Prakrama's death the quarrels of his successors had once more reduced the Sinhalese to ruin. Calinga invaders took advantage of the confusion, and Lanka fell for ever from its place in the sun. On three successive occasions Prakrama's widow, Lilivati, ascended the throne, only to be deposed each time.

172. Despairing of Polonnaruwa, Wijaya Bahu III, made his capital at Dambedeniya in 1235, but his harassed successors moved ever deeper into the mountains, and further and further to the south. The Sinhalese, distracted by external enemies and internal feuds, were a broken race. Upon the fertile northern plain the jungle spread over field and garden, palace, and temple. The neglected waterworks degenerated into mere swamps. Mosquitoes completed what the Malabaris had begun.

## CHAPTER VIII

### YAPAHUWA

And Other Capitals of Despair

173. Yapahuwa is a site which deserves better attention than it receives. Its proximity to the railway makes it easy to reach ; but these ruins are eclipsed by the fame of the older capitals, and for this reason, few travellers turn aside from the beaten path of monuments that have a world-wide reputation. Still, it is a pity. There is a magnificent stairway at Yapahuwa, and though the sight-seeing is more or less limited to these steps, they are considered by experts to be of high artistic importance. The surrounding country also is attractive.

174. After the destruction of Polonnaruwa, the Sinhalese never again achieved greatness. Dambedeniya was abandoned and another capital was founded at Yapahuwa. Yapahuwa is a rock-fastness that rises boldly from the plain three miles from the present railway junction at Maho. On all sides (apparently) its walls rise in forbidding precipices, and it could easily have been rendered as impregnable as Sigiriya. Here, for the second time in history, a Sinhalese capital was founded on the brow of a

cliff ; and King Bhuwaneka Bahu I, like Kassiyappa before him at Sigiriya, took his stand in a rock-fortress. This, the last seat of a united Sinhalese Government, survived for only eleven years from A.D. 1303. Then the remorseless Pandyan overthrew it, and the Sinhalese thereafter degenerated into a number of petty principalities. It is interesting to contemplate what the race might have accomplished in the way of architecture if it had been left in peace—but the speculation is idle ; for the fate of the Sinhalese has been the fate of many other artistic people since the days of Egypt and Greece.

175. There is something very pitiful about this last desperate effort at Yapahuwa. The selection of a cramped hill-top by a nation whose former capitals had spread luxuriously across the plains was in itself the choice of despair. And instead of directing their energies to repelling an implacable foe, thoughtless princes set out upon a programme of architectural feats which remain to this day a monument to their levity. True, little was effected in the way of buildings at Yapahuwa ; but considering the conditions, and the short period for which the city survived, it is surprising that anything at all was achieved. And certainly, the Sinhalese Government could have been better employed than in erecting a monumental staircase.

176. These steps consisted originally of three flights close together, and all near the foot of the mountain. But the central flight has disappeared, and has been replaced by one of those horrid, dizzy ladders beloved by the Archæological Department. The upper flight is the most splendid of all, and is really worth going a long way to see. The whole structure is built of granulite. The style is Hindu, and strongly reminiscent of that of Siva Devale I at Polonnaruwa: for the same lotus-petal 'dentation' occurs. The balustrades are heavily ornamented with lions, dragons, elephants, and other devices, including the composite beast *gaja-sinha*, half lion, half elephant. The lions are after the style of the familiar 'Celestial dogs' frequently seen on Chinese stairways. These grand steps culminate in a gate, or porch, embellished with graceful pillars. The gate is chaste and simple, and rectangular in shape: and so are the window spaces which flank it.

177. From these ruins at Yapahuwa, was recovered a perforated stone trellis, or window, which has been considered of the highest artistic merit. It is now preserved in the Colombo Museum.

178. The rest of the ascent to the summit of the hill is a scramble up clefts, and over bare rock, where rough steps have been cut when necessary. But though steep, the climb offers no difficulties whatever,

YAPAHUWA

These monumental stairs are considered to be of great artistic merit. The capital at Yapahuwa survived only 11 years from A.D. 1303.

*Facing page* 108

and is much less 'giddy' than the ascent to Sigiriya. It is also surprisingly short, considering the apparent height of the cliffs. At the summit there are ruins of a comparatively modern pagoda, and traces of a tank, and of a building called Raja Maligawa, which is supposed to have been the palace. But these remains are of little interest. The site was excavated in 1912, and proved disappointing. The view, however, is magnificent. The surrounding country is intriguing. Many other peaks are seen, and of these one points a rocky finger into the sky.

179. The city, of course, lay at the foot of the hill. Its walls can still be traced, and one ruin, the Pansala, survives in a fair state of preservation. But the fortifications were not able to save the capital from Nemesis. After the death of Bhuwaneka Bahu, Yapahuwa fell in about A.D. 1314: and the Pandyans captured not only the citadel, but, what was an even greater disaster, they gained possession of the 'Tooth Relic,' and carried it off to India. It is hard for us to realize now what a national calamity this must have been. Subsequently, the Sinhalese ransomed the 'Tooth': but Yapahuwa was abandoned in A.D. 1319 in favour of a site still further to the south at Kurunegala, under the shelter of the Kandyan Hills.

. . . . .

180. Kurunegala is one of the few old capitals which has achieved importance in modern times. It lies on the railway, and is the residence of many wealthy and influential Sinhalese. The country round about is one vast palm garden, and the town itself lies buried in the foliage of coco-nuts and rain trees. Above all these rises one of those flawless hills which are nothing more or less than single boulders of gigantic proportions. Its black, granite cliffs are seen from a hundred aspects, rising above the foliage, or set off against a blazing mass of gold-mohur. The climb to the top of this rock past the Kachcheri, and up over rounded, naked rock, to the Ibbagala Pagoda, is a charming excursion. Higher still there is jungle, the haunt of *Memnon parinda* and other handsome butterflies: and from the summit, where the cliffs fall sheer to the plain, a glorious panorama of Kandyan Hill is unfolded. Many of the neighbouring peaks are bold and picturesque, and at their feet nestles a rich country of rice fields and coco-nut. Two beautiful lakes—and no Sinhalese countryside is complete without its lakes—sparkle in the sunshine. Few landscapes in Ceylon are more pleasing.

181. As far as I could ascertain, there are no important ruins in the vicinity, and modern Kurunegala has quite forgotten that it was ever a short-time capital.

It could not have held this distinction for long, for by 1410 a capital was established at Cotta (now a suburb of Colombo). Two years before that (in 1408) a Chinese force invaded the Island and carried off King Vijaya Bahu IV, as a punishment for some insult offered to a Celestial Envoy. In 1505 (or as some now say, 1506), d'Almedia landed, and Ceylon passed definitely to a new phase—that arising from European intercourse.

## CHAPTER IX

### EUROPEAN OCCUPATIONS

182. The advent of the Portuguese inaugurates the rediscovery of Ceylon by Europe. Sources of information now become fixed, thanks to a series of Portuguese maps, and to later Dutch adaptions. Francesco Berlinghieri's *Atlas* of 1480, based on that of Ptolemy, still failed to show India as a peninsula, and Ceylon is still represented as a great land mass. It was, however, now known to be an island and is called 'Taprobane Isola,' with the southern mountains marked 'Malea.' The Roman *Geographia* of ten years later (A.D. 1490) shows hardly any improvement: but Lafreri's *Roman Atlas* of 1572, though still based on Ptolemy's, is a great advance. This was the best map of the century. India is developed into a peninsula, and 'Isola de Zeilan' though still crude in shape, is more correct as regards its size. Lafreri's work is the first progressive step in fourteen hundred years. According to Mr. E. Reimers, Government Archivist,[1] the 16th-century map by Petrus Plancius "gave a fair presentation of the western and southern coast-lines, but suggested a poor

[1] *Ceylon Daily News*: 6th June, 1927.

knowledge of the east and north of the island. The mountain system, as in all the maps mentioned above, is given extraordinary prominence, and Adam's Peak is shown towering above its lesser brethren." A map of Ceylon appearing in a block edition of Spilburgen's *First Voyage to the East Indies* (1601–4) curiously transposes the east and west coasts. "One of the most prominent objects is 'Pagoda Grande,' probably the famous temple of Dewinuwera or Dondra."

183. But the most important advance was the Dutch copy of a Portuguese 'book of maps' compiled in 1629, with descriptive letterpress. "This," says Mr. Reimers, "was a distinct improvement in shape on the earlier map of Petrus Plancius."

184. Persistent ill-fortune dogged the Portuguese in all their ventures in Ceylon. Their purpose was twofold—the acquisition of worldly wealth, and the dissemination of spiritual grace: and in either cause they were prepared to stick at nothing. Of the first arrivals nothing is known except that they carved the date 1501 on a rock which is now preserved in Colombo: d'Almedia's visit in 1505 was accidental. The Portuguese did not seriously turn their attention to the Island till twelve years later.

185. At that period, Jaffna in the north was already in the hands of Malabar Indians. In the south,

Prakrama Bahu IX ruled at Cotta near the modern Colombo: but the unity of the Sinhalese was gone, and there were minor and independent kings at Badulla, Gampola, Mahagam, Peradeniya, and Kandy. In these circumstances, the Portuguese had plenty of scope for playing off one chief against another: and in a short time Prakrama Bahu IX and his successors had been reduced to Christianity and to a state of entire dependence on the foreign guns at Colombo. As the power of the Chiefs waned, so the scorn and hatred of their people grew, until the nationalist movement assumed active shape with the Hill Sinhalese under Maaya Dunnai, the Chief of Kandy. The plains were constantly ravaged, Cotta was frequently besieged. The impotent Sinhalese King—now Bhuwaneka VII—was so estranged from his people that the succession of his heir was only secured by sending the boy's effigy to Lisbon, where it was solemnly crowned in 1541, and given the title of Don Juan.

186. In 1544 a punitive expedition was sent against Jaffna, which was repeated in 1560. This was the occasion when the 'Tooth Relic,' which happened to have been sent to Jaffna for safety, fell into the hands of the Portuguese, and was by them publicly destroyed. Meanwhile, the authority of Don Juan hardly extended beyond the walls of Colombo: and the country

was being ravaged by spasmodic warfare. In 1548, and again in 1550, Portuguese forces marching on Kandy were cut to pieces. In 1571 the old Sinhalese Chief of Kandy was succeeded by his still more able son Raja Sinha, who dealt summarily with waverers, and besieged Colombo itself, reducing the garrison to the verge of cannibalism.[1] By a skilful political deal, however, the tables were turned. Kandy was seized in 1582: but in '86 Raja Sinha was back before Colombo. It was to distract the attention of this persistent foe, that the Portuguese now sent expeditions to ravage the neighbouring coast; and of these expeditions the second one sacked and demolished the sacred temple whose ruins may still be seen near the Dondra Head Lighthouse. Appalled by this tragedy, Raja Sinha raised the siege, and success thereafter deserted him. Kandy was taken: and then Don Juan—he whose effigy had been crowned at Lisbon—suddenly discarded his nonentity. He deserted the Portuguese, embraced Buddhism, assumed the title of Wimala Dharma, produced another 'Tooth Relic' out of his pocket, and became King of Kandy. Now, Kandy had been earmarked by the Portuguese for the daughter of a previous king. She was a good Catholic, and her name was Donna Catharina. They took up arms in her cause against

[1] Tennent's *Ceylon*, Vol. II, page 17.

the faithless Don Juan (now Wimala Dharma). He was defeated, but won the odd trick by bribery. Henceforth, he became the most influential Chief in Ceylon. The exasperated Portuguese now continued the struggle under the villainous Jerome Azavedu, whose barbarities included the slaughter of women and babies with every appropriate refinement. It was this devil who made a pun about Galle while massacring its children—"How the young *Gallos* (cocks) crow." The name Galle is popularly supposed to be derived from this incident, but as a matter of fact it is really a corruption of the Sinhalese *Galla*, a rock.

187. In the midst of this butchery Don Juan (King Wimala Dharma) died in 1597, and as a last saving act of grace "bequeathed his dominions by will to Phillip II of Spain." (Spain by this time had seized Portugal.) To this surprising bequest, the Sinhalese Chiefs acquiesced ; though they politely declined an offer of wholesale baptism. Jaffna, of course, remained with the Malabaris ; and Kandy preserved its independence to the end, and advertised it by occasional raids into the Portuguese coastal provinces. Colombo became the seat of Portuguese Government, but of course the past disturbances had eaten up all the profits of trade. Galle also rose to prominence on account of its harbour, and Kalutara

and Negombo flourished as cinnamon growing areas. In 1617 the Portuguese at last took Jaffna.

. . . . .

188. In the meantime Holland, as far back as 1580, had thrown off the Spanish yoke, and had embarked upon her maritime enterprise. The peaceful distribution to Europe of Portuguese Oriental merchandise, offered an outlet to her energies, till the Spanish masters of Portugal, foolishly placed obstructions in the way. Then the Dutch found a route to the East for themselves, where they soon came into conflict with the Portuguese, who, as Vassals of Spain, were fair game. The Dutch landed at Trincomalee in 1602, and sent a mission to the King of Kandy, who welcomed them with open arms as a possible ally against the hated Portuguese. The King had married Donna Catharina, who, when he died, succeeded him ; and a formal Dutch-Sinhalese alliance was agreed to in 1609. The Dutch built a fort at Trincomalee in 1612, but the Portuguese destroyed it : and Holland, being temporarily in disfavour, a Portuguese-Sinhalese pact resulted ; and in 1622 and 1627 the Portuguese fortified Trincomalee and Batticaloa. Thenceforth the contest became three-cornered, since both the Portuguese and Sinhalese were rank opportunists. In 1630 a Portuguese force was cut up near Badulla ; and Raja Sinha II (with temporary Dutch

sympathies), having succeeded at Kandy, an agreement was made as the result of which the Dutch Admiral Westerwold appeared in 1638. Batticaloa, Trincomalee, Negombo, Matara, and Galle fell to the Dutch. Colombo was invested by the Sinhalese, and might have been captured also had not the Kandy Chief become alarmed at the growing power of his Dutch ally. A truce followed, which ended at the outbreak of war in Europe in 1650: and in 1655 and 1656 the Dutch took Kalutara and Colombo, following up these successes with the capture of Jaffna. The Portuguese were thus eliminated.

189. Hostilities, however, continued between Holland and Kandy. In 1664 a British Mission appeared at Kandy to negotiate the release of captive sailors. The Dutch meanwhile turned their attention to trade. Throughout their dealings with Ceylon, they had shown a reluctance for war, and an extraordinary patience even in the face of grave provocation. Nevertheless, the prosperity of the indigenous people was not one of their concerns. Their whole residence of nearly a century and a half was frankly a military occupation. Ceylon was of strategic value to Holland's other possessions, and its chief importance in the eyes of the Dutch lay in that. Despairing of friendship with Kandy, they planted cinnamon for themselves in the plains, and enlarged their forts to

protect the rich plantations. Unfortunately, the cost of these armaments was excessive, and there was an annual deficit in revenue. In 1672 war broke out with France, and a French squadron (eagerly welcomed by the Sinhalese) took Trincomalee and Batticaloa, but was unable to maintain itself.

190. In Kandy, Raja Sinha II died in 1687; and his successors Wimala Dharma II and Koondasala, devoted themselves to a religious revival—Buddhism having been once more nearly extinguished during the recent turmoil. With the help of the Dutch, Buddhist priests from Arakan were once again brought over to conduct the necessary ordinations. But on the death of Koondasala in 1739, the Sinhalese dynasty became extinct; and a Malabar prince, a brother of the late Queen, succeeded. In 1782 the British took Trincomalee, but were evicted by a French fleet, the troops being ignominously taken back to Madras whence they came.

191. By 1795 Holland herself had been seized by the armies of the French Republic, and as Napoleon's Vassal was soon involved in a war with England. In that same year a British Expedition from Madras, under Colonel James Stuart, landed at Trincomalee. The place was taken in three weeks. Negombo and Colombo fell in quick succession, and the remaining

Dutch possessions in Ceylon were formally surrendered.

. . . . .

192. At first attached to Madras, Ceylon became a Crown Colony in 1798: and the position was regularized by the Treaty of Amiens in 1803, whereby the Malay Archipelago was defined as the proper zone for Dutch enterprise.

For a while British influence was limited to the coast, the interior of the Island being in the hands of the Indian King of Kandy, whose treacherous minister was plotting to seize the throne. In these intrigues the British Government was soon entangled, and indeed, it may be admitted that the situation was very perplexing. Unfortunately, a vacillating policy only led to worse confusion. Another King was supported and then abandoned, and finally the British were committed to a troublesome war with the Sinhalese in 1803. Kandy was easily occupied, but proved unhealthy, and all the troops were withdrawn except a small garrison of a thousand Europeans and Malays, with a hospital filled with 150 sick. The command of this ill-fated force devolved on Major Davie, who seems to have lacked even the rudimentary qualities of a soldier. The Kandyans having been left unmolested, soon besieged the camp. Davie capitulated under promise of safe-conduct, and surrendered the sick. Very soon afterwards he allowed himself and most of his officers to be drawn into a conference where he was captured. The leaderless troops were then decoyed across a river in batches by the Kandyans, and butchered in detail. The surrendered sick met a like fate. It is in fact a story of amazing irresolution. Major Davie himself remained a prisoner at Kandy for seven years till his death in 1810.

193. Emboldened by these extraordinary successes, the Kandyans soon pressed down towards the maritime provinces. In 1804 the incompetent military authorities planned an invasion of Kandy, but abandoned it. They failed, however, to cancel the orders of Captain Johnson, and this resolute officer not only took Kandy alone and unsupported, but fought his small detachment safely out again, thus proving the real rottenness of the enemy's troops. Nevertheless, nothing further occurred for eleven years—this period being employed by the British in fruitless negotiations, and by the King of Kandy in a disastrous quarrel with his strong and unscrupulous nobles. Sri Vikrama Raja Sinha was probably not the out-and-out tyrant that history has painted him. He was a foreigner. But he seems genuinely to have wished to shield his subjects from the harshness of their own chiefs. It was this that roused the latters' hostility. Further, the king probably failed to appreciate the character of

the British with whom he had now to deal, instead of with Portuguese or Dutch.

194. In 1815, the new Governor, Sir Robert Brownrigg, determined to put an end to this state of things. He declared war, and within a month the King was captured and exiled, while the Kandyan Chiefs formally transferred their allegiance to the British Crown. In this they were not departing at all from precedent. Ceylon, as we have seen, had on one occasion been left to Phillip of Spain : and it had been a custom to obviate disputes in the island by bringing over foreign kings from India. But seeing that their ancient privileges were suffering under the new regime, the Chiefs rebelled in 1817. The rebellion proved formidable. It quickly spread, and lasted for nine months, involving much loss of life and property.

195. The tenure of the next Governor, Sir Edward Barnes, was devoted to the restoration of law and order, and to the construction of roads and bridges. Proper administration was now extended to the whole island. In 1831 forced labour, after having lasted two thousand years, was abolished. Schools were opened; and the freedom of individuals was guaranteed by a charter. So did Ceylon enter into the way of peace.

## CHAPTER X

## SINHALESE INFLUENCE ABROAD

### The Spread of Buddhism

196. The introduction of Buddhism into Ceylon in the third century B.C. was an event that has profoundly influenced the destinies of Southern Asia. A philosophy so wise, so benevolent, has never failed to mitigate the natural ferocity of the human animal: and if, instead of curbing passion, it has sometimes produced a sort of fatalism, that is only because men have adopted it merely in the letter and not in the spirit. For centuries it has been misunderstood and misinterpreted by priest and layman alike. That has been the fate of other revelations also: but Buddhism, as it left the Master's lips, must have been a clear and simple appeal that arrested immediate attention. Otherwise it could not have inspired such widespread response. To-day, through the fog of ignorance and superstition, we hear but an echo of that message: yet, it is sufficient to have "made our Asia mild."

197. In India, Buddhism did not long survive the death of Asoka. Having succumbed to the hostility of the Brahmans, it soon degenerated into a crude

Shamanistic devil worship, and in that form was introduced into Tibet and China. In that form also it first reached Burma, Siam, and Cambodia.

198. It is this that lends significance to the fact that the lamp of pure Hinayana Buddhism was lit in Ceylon by Mahinda in 307 B.C., and that, in spite of flickerings, it has continued to shine (though now dimly) for all the world to see. In the 1st century B.C. the Law, which hitherto had been passed down orally for four hundred years, was committed to writing by order of King Walagam Bahu at the Rock Temple of Alu-wihara, and from that time Ceylon has been the source from which many countries have derived their religion, and at which they have sought information and instruction from time to time.

199. One of the first countries to receive Buddhism (at least partially) from Ceylon was Southern Burma, which in the early centuries of our era was inhabited by a Mongoloid race called Mon. Their capital at Thaton was one of the gates through which, at a very early date, and before the dawn of authentic history, Burma received her literature, architecture and pure southern Buddhism. Thaton now 20 miles from the sea, was then a port of a country known as Ramanya. Ramanya included Thaton, Hanthawaddy, Muttama (Martaban), and Kuthein (the modern Pathein, or Bassein). It is popularly believed that Asoka sent

the missionaries Sona and Outtara to Thaton in 306 B.C. There is, however, no proof at all that Buddhism was introduced so early, or until the beginning of our era. The adoption of this myth by authoritative writers illustrates the danger of an uncritical acceptance of legend. The mission to Burma or Suvannabhumi (which term, by the way, embraces the whole coast from Hanoi and Malaya to Bassein) is indeed mentioned in *Mahawansa* (Chapter XII), and on that venerable authority has been accepted by men like Bigandet and Forchhammer. But, as Duroiselle has since pointed out, the Sinhalese of A.D. 500 could not read Asoka's edicts: and those edicts, so precise and exact in detail, are now found to contain no reference whatever to the supposed mission to Burma. We may, however, accept the fact that a missionary, or missionaries, came to Burma at some early period, and probably from Ceylon, but not till long after Asoka's time.[1]

200. Buddhism was probably introduced into Burma orally: and there is another popular legend to the effect that the written text was brought from Ceylon in A.D. 400 by Buddha Ghosa. One of the caves at Alu-wihara, as we have seen, is dedicated to him, and Burmese pilgrims are fond of visiting it. Unfortunately, even Buddha Ghosa's mission to

[1] Enriquez' *A Burmese Wonderland*, page 18.

Burma is now questioned: but in any case, the Lopburi inscription show that Mons (better known as Talaings) wrote and used Pali and Sanskrit words in the 6th and 7th centuries A.D.[1]

201. Buddhism in Ceylon has survived, without a break, since its introduction. But, as we have seen, it was beset with heresies at an early date: and the Anuradhapura period was filled with disputes between the orthodox Hinayanist priests and the heretical ones of Mahayana, who were ready and anxious to adopt any sort of slack or subversive doctrine. Nearly all these innovations tended towards the relaxation of priestly discipline. The Mahayanists, or as they were called the *Dhammaruci*, were a strong party with rich endowments; and in the reign of Maha Sen (A.D. 275–302) they so far excelled, that the orthodox priests fled from the capital in a body. The King, who had pandered to the heretical priests, now returned to the old faith—possibly in deference to public opinion. Disturbances of this kind were probably semi-political, and their importance may be inferred from Fa Hien's estimate that in the 5th century the priests numbered from fifty to sixty thousand. These early disputes are significant because they seriously weakened Buddhism, and the taint of indiscipline remains to this day. Even now, the

[1] Enriquez' *A Burmese Wonderland*, page 19.

priests of Burma and Ceylon do not all observe their vows of celibacy.

202. Ambitious voyages were made across the Indian Ocean at a very early date. In Java, Hinduism was introduced in the first century of our era, but in the 5th century Buddhism took root—Buddhism of the Hinayanist type, which we may suppose was of Sinhalese origin, since it came to Java from Sumatra. Sumatra, we know, from the writings of the Chinese historian Chao Ju, had a colony in Ceylon.

This Hindu-Buddhist civilization expressed itself in the great temples of Brambanan and Boro Bodeo, and left a deep and lasting impression on the history, literature and society of Java. In the 5th century also, we find Fa Hien visiting Ceylon ; and Chinese pilgrims studied, and copied books, in the island for the next two hundred years.

203. Cambodia received Hinayana Buddhism much later. Whatever Mahayanist forms it may originally have possessed, were submerged early in our era by Hinduism. The Khmer reached the zenith of their power under Jayavarman III. The royal city of Angkor Thom was completed about A.D. 900 : and in the 10th century Buddhism superseded Hinduism. The great temple of Angkor Vat probably dates from the beginning of the 12th century. But here we must return to Ceylon.

204. During the Tamil invasions that had culminated in the abandonment of Anuradhapura, Buddhism had suffered so severely that indeed it had been almost extinguished. When King Vijaya Bahu (A.D. 1071) had expelled the enemy, and restored the capital at Polonnaruwa, he found the priesthood so depleted that it was impossible to conduct the authorized forms of ordination. In this difficulty he turned to Burma, where the religion had recently undergone one of the most remarkable revivals in its history.

205. Fourteen years previously (A.D. 1057) Anawratta (the Burmese Napoleon) having ascended the throne, raided the old Talaing capital at Thaton, carried off its books, priests, and architects, and then proceeded to turn his Burmese capital at Pågān into a great Buddhist metropolis. Anawratta had none of the finer Buddhist sentiments, but he developed the fanaticism of a convert; and he soon turned his attention to the degraded Shamanistic priests who, before this revival had flourished at Pågān. They were there called *Ari*, and they had much the same pretensions as the *Dhammaruci* of Ceylon. The *Ari* had probably been introduced from Bengal in the 6th century, and were occupying themselves with sorcery, alchemy and animal sacrifice. Among their immoralities, they even claimed the right of *jus primae noctis*, or violating brides, and it is probably

this that brought down upon them the wrath of Anawratta. He suppressed them : but unfortunately this persecution only scattered them over the country, or drove them underground.

206. These abuses—notably the *jus primae noctis*—continued up to the 13th century amongst certain priests in Siam, Laos, and Cambodia, and are believed still to exist amongst the Hkamti Shans of Burma. According to Harvey's *History of Burma*, they were exercised by the *Myothugyis* of Popa (Central Burma) up till three generations ago. Like Maha Sen in Ceylon, King Alaungsithu of Burma continued to countenance the heresy, which was still largely political ; and the *Ari* suffered no further check till the religious movement under King Dhammacheti in the 15th century, and until a hundred years later King Hsinbyu Shin prohibited intoxicating offerings and bloody sacrifices. The last direct mention of the *Ari* occurs in the 14th century, when, at Pinya (Ava), they are represented as soldier-priests. But in Burma, as in Ceylon, the old spirit survives, and is at the bottom of half the lawlessness and depravity amongst certain sections of the priesthood.

207. Thus we see how natural it was for Vijaya Bahu I to relight the torch of Sinhalese Buddhism from Burma. In return he sent to that country a 'duplicate' of the Tooth which was landed at Law-

kananda near Pāgān. King Anawratta met it in state, placed it on an elephant; and where the elephant stopped, enshrined the relic in his now famous Shwezigon Pagoda. So we have a direct connection between Polonnaruwa and Burma's celebrated shrine —the Shwezigon. At both capitals an orgy of pagoda building was about to break out.

208. Vijaya's successor, Prakrama (A.D. 1153–80), was also a revivalist: and under his patronage Buddhism resumed its ancient sovereignty in Ceylon. Like Anawratta just a century before him, he dealt summarily with the heresy, and as far as can be ascertained, this is the last heard of it in Ceylon. However, Hindu influence had greatly increased, and at least two shrines at Polonnaruwa are frankly Hindu. Traces of this Hinduism are also evident at Pāgān. At the end of Prakrama's reign, or soon afterwards, King Narapatisithu of Burma (A.D. 1173–1210) sent a priestly mission to Ceylon. It was headed by Uttarajiva who took with him a young monk called Chapada. Chapada remained ten years, and returned to Burma 'well equipped to teach the Law.' His Sinhalese training is immediately apparent from the small pagoda (the Chapada) which he built when he got home to Pāgān. Above the dome is the characteristic box-like structure of Ceylon.

209. In 1281, Kublai Khan obtained two teeth of

Buddha, and a lock of Adam's hair.[1] Such gifts were marks of special favour, and the recipients always accepted them with profound respect.

210. We have now to turn to Siam where, according to tradition, a form of Mon or Talaing Buddhism, had been introduced at Lampun. It was spread thence to Northern Siam by Princess Cham Thewi of Lawo (Lopburi) in the 7th century. Lopburi was first a Mon, and then a Khmer capital: and in Ayudhyan (Siamese) times was a summer residence of Siamese Kings. The Siamese, it should be understood, are a sort of slow growth out of Shan and Khmer elements, which only assumed shape in the 13th century during the decay of Angkor. Southern Buddhism was not introduced till the 14th and 15th centuries, when much priestly intercourse between Ceylon and Northern Siam is on record.

211. In 1560, the Portuguese captured Jaffna from the Tamils, and so came into possession of the Tooth Relic which had been sent there for safety during a period of commotion in the Sinhalese States. The Portuguese carried it to Goa, and we find King Bayin Naung of Pegu offering to buy it for 8 lakhs of rupees. The offer was refused, and the Relic destroyed. Nevertheless it rose miraculously into the air and returned to Ceylon, whence it was

[1] Knox's *History of Ceylon*, page 11.

sent to Bayin Naung in 1576. He met it at Bassein in state, and enshrined it in the Mahazedi Pagoda at Păgān. He considered the acquisition of the Tooth as the crowning event of his life. There are none so blind as those who do not wish to see.

212. In about 1730, Buddhism, having been once more nearly extinguished during the Dutch and Portuguese wars, we find Ceylon again so depleted of priests that application had to be made to Burma. This was in the reign of the Sinhalese King Koondasala. A few years later a Burmese King, Hsinbyu Shin (A.D. 1763–75) built a distinctly Sinhalese Pagoda, the Hsin-mya Shin at Sagaing (Upper Burma). It is a stupa, surmounted by the characteristic 'box' of Ceylon: the whole structure being supported by a fresco of elephants. It is very evidently a small-scale replica of the Ruanweli at Anuradhapura —or was, until a misdirected restoration in about 1920 destroyed its original design.

213. This marks the close of direct Sinhalese influence abroad. Troubles at home had overwhelmed Ceylon, and the now feeble Government had been chased from one capital to another by the remorseless Pandyan. Indirect relations, however, continue to this day; and Ceylon, the ancient, the venerable, is still looked to by all Buddhist nations as their Spiritual Home, just as the nations of Europe look to Rome.

214. There is, after all, nothing in the least bit extraordinary in all the intercourse which we have here described between Ceylon and her neighbours. We are apt to suppose that the high seas were impassable before the advent of the P. and O. and Bibby. But formerly there were other routes and other means, sufficient at least for the adventurous, in days when time was of less consequence, and men had not yet learned to travel *de luxe*. The crazy sailing ships we still see leaving Trinco for Madras, Rangoon and Moulmein, are merely the descendants of ancient dhows whose crews had learned, centuries ago, to avail themselves of the calm winds of the Bay. Just as to-day I and Maung Ba Kye (my Burmese servant) are taking back to Burma a leaf of the Bo Tree, a picture post card of Thuparama, and a book full of incoherent notes, so have Burmese, Chinese, Javanese, Siamese, and Malays carried away impressions of Ceylon since the days of Chapada and Fa Hien. There is nothing new in it, nothing wonderful. But possibly those leisurely adventurers of old were better travellers than ourselves. Perhaps their observations were less superficial.

# BOOK II

# CEYLON—PRESENT

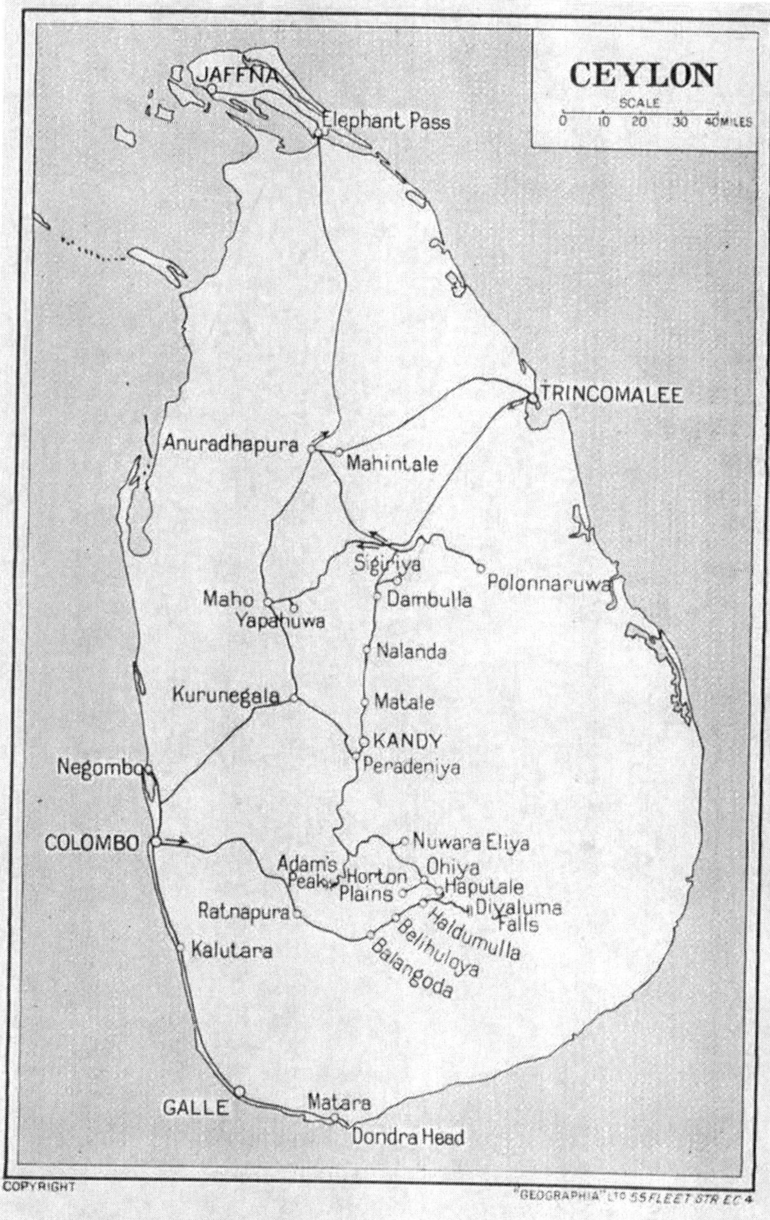


*Facing page 136*

## CHAPTER XI

### THE SOUTH COAST

#### The Old Dutch Towns

215. The atmosphere of the south coast towns of Ceylon is still largely Dutch. Few traces of Portuguese occupation survive: and at Negombo, that Garden of the 'Fragrant Cinnamon,' only a gate remains even of the Dutch fort which was built in 1678, and which Tennent reported eighty years ago as "in effective repair." A few Dutch houses, however, are preserved, notably that now assigned to the Assistant Government Agent which dates from 1680, and is believed to have been a salt godown. The Dutch church which stood within the enclosure of the cemetery was probably demolished early in the last century—another victim of thoughtless Vandalism.

216. The cemetery contains the grave, now in a ruinous state, of Thomas Hetherington, of His Majesty's 52nd Regiment, who is stated to have died at Negombo the 6th day of February, 1796. As a matter of fact, he must have died at sea; for the Dutch did not surrender Negombo to the British till the 9th. Colombo fell exactly a week later. This British grave is therefore the earliest one after the occupation. The first known English monument,

however, is that of a Naval Captain whose ship touched at Trincomalee in 1748. There are, according to J. P. Lewis[1], only five British graves of the 18th century in Ceylon. About a week before my visit to Negombo a steam-roller accidently broke into fragments a beautifully carved slab that stood in the gateway of the Dutch fort, the inscription of which begins : '*IBI CINNAMOMI ODORANTIS.*'

217. The Negombo coast is partly sea, partly lagoon. The lagoon forms a network of inland creeks and waterways, which flow out to sea rather swiftly when the tide falls. This outflow has thrown up a bar opposite the shore, so that the water within, though not always salt, is at least protected from sharks. On the other hand, the current is strong, so that bathers have to be careful. Add to all this a sandy beach, a palm-fringed coast, and a Rest House that has all the amenities of a good hotel, and you have a picture of Negombo, the justly popular health resort of Ceylon. It is essentially a place for prawn curry and fresh fish ; and indeed, the fishing operations of the natives are the chief excitement of the day. Picturesque *catamarangs*, with square, red sails, go out at dusk to lay the nets, and in the dawn return laden with the spoils of a tropical sea. The bulk of the catch usually consists of crabs and lobsters :

[1] J. P. Lewis' *Tombstones and Monuments in Ceylon.*

Plâté

NEGOMBO

They return laden at dawn with the spoils of a tropical sea.

*Facing page 138*

but sharks, running up to four feet in length, are frequently brought in. If the weather is at all rough, the fishermen go out on boat-shaped rafts made of three or four coco-nut planks, and on these they ride the surf of the bar. It is very amusing to watch these rafts sweeping in on the crest of a wave. The fish are usually sold on the beach, after the Church has taken its tithe—for all these naked fisherfolk have been good Catholics since the gently persuasive occupation of the Portuguese.

218. It has always struck me as curious that rich countries like Ceylon and Malaya which can afford to indulge a taste for Museums and so on, have never created Aquariums. Situated as they are by tropical seas, which teem with all manner of extraordinary fish, they could so easily establish aquariums of intense interest, and of great educational and scientific value.

219. A curious phenomenon is sometimes seen off this coast, when the sea is invaded by a red colour. I have witnessed it near Colombo. The dividing line between the red water and the blue is so sharp, that it seems as if a current, or a river, was discharging mud. But, as a matter of fact, this red colour is due to the presence of millions of tiny *infusoria*.

. . . . .

220. Of Colombo it is hardly necessary to say anything, beyond the fact that it is a Den of Thieves.

Coolies and touts are allowed to clamour for a wage exceeding that received by a commissioned Indian Officer in the Army: and they get it. As a result of these importunities the significance and relative value of money is lost. I was actually offered a dead scorpion there for Rs.12—a thing which I have no desire whatever to possess, at any price. But I suppose even the corpse of a scorpion may be a welcome distraction to a thoroughly bored tourist. I concur with the policy of making idle Globe Trotters pay: but of the travellers who put in at Colombo, there are many who are just 'Servants' and Exiles in the East, passing upon their lawful occasions. Without commenting on the honesty of the attitude of "Here is a Stranger —rob him," I would merely point out, in all friendliness, that that sort of thing is demoralizing, and cultivates a pimping community such as disgraces Port Said. There are in Colombo hostels, frankly and openly, two tariffs—one for Residents who cannot be bamboozled and one for Strangers who can.

221. For the rest, Colombo, that Queen of the Tropic Seas, needs no panegyric. Her attractive and flowery roads, the palms by a summer sea, the breezes and twinkling lights of her Esplanade—who has not fallen under their spell? Who is there, amongst those who come up from the sea, who has not been refreshed and gladdened by the glittering gaiety of her hotels?

Plâté

A PALM-FRINGED COAST

Some are straight and stately, some tortured by the wind of many monsoons, and others again reach out yearningly towards the sea.

*Facing page 140*

And Mt. Lavinia is known to all the world. Alas, that so many travellers, yearning for Home and England, pass this Island by, with only a glance at these superficial aspects. Colombo is but the gate of a lovely and mysterious fairyland.

. . . . .

222. The whole coast from Colombo to Galle and Matara is fringed with palms. There is probably no other part of the world where the coco-nut flourishes so luxuriantly as in the sandy soil and humid air of southern Ceylon. The natives recognize three varieties of fruit, which range in colour from golden-orange to dark green. The beauty of these miles of coco-nut is saved from monotony by an endless variety in the grouping of the trees along strips of yellow sand, or upon headlands and islands. The palms also have each their own individuality—some straight and stately, some tortured by the wind of many monsoons, and others again reaching out yearningly towards the sea. Through the tracery of their million slender trunks, are seen the long green waves of the Indian Ocean which come tumbling in upon the coral beach in lines of curling, breaking water. The south-west Monsoon beats upon the coast with a never-ceasing thunder.

223. Beneath the palms, the shadows are deep and restful; and in that quiet shade thatched huts and

villages are scattered all up and down the coast. At frequent intervals there are little towns, whose busy appearance suggests that they are still very much alive, in spite of the old-world Dutch style of their architecture. Such are Kalutara, Bentota, and Ambalangoda. Usually these towns are situated at the mouths of rivers. And so, at length, you come to Galle.

. . . . .

224. Galle is undoubtedly a port of great antiquity. The Arabs used it for their trade between Venice and the Malay Archipelago : and, according to Tennent,[1] it was the ' Kalah ' at which the Arabians in the time of Haroun al Raschid met the junks of the Chinese, and " brought back gems, silks and spices from Serendib." Some say that it was from Ceylon that came those lovely pearl-encrusted fabrics that were the delight of the ultra-modern patrician ladies of ancient Rome.[2]

225. Apart from the native town, from which it is separated by a green expanse of lawn, Galle may be said to be the old Dutch fort which occupies a promontory, and faces the sea on three sides. This fort is a noble building, with ramparts quite a mile and a half in circumference. All the important buildings

[1] Tennent's *Ceylon*, Vol. II, page 100.

[2] E. Reimer, Government Archivist, *Ceylon Daily News*, 6th June, 1927.

of Galle lie within it, grouped in 'quarters'—one quarter for the English, one for the Burghers, one for the Sinhalese, one for the Mahommedans, and so on. The Mahommedans are numerous and from an early date Galle has been the resort of Moorish jewellers who have now bought up the hotels and hostels, and converted them into private residences. The Dutch church stands in the very centre of the fort. It contains a number of interesting old monuments, but many of these have been brought together from other sites, and some are older than the church itself.

226. Most of the offices and stores, as their spacious architecture suggests, are of Dutch origin. The Arms of Holland are still seen above the principal gate, whose original doors are yet on their hinges. (The entrance to the fort from the direction of the station is said to be comparatively modern.) The Queen's House, now used by high Government officials, is mentioned by Tennent on his arrival as having been lent to him by Sir Colin Campbell in 1845.

227. The fortress, of course, is built of stone; but the ramparts are now capped with soft green turf. The walls are protected from the assault of the ocean by barriers of rock which form a natural breakwater. Here, the south-west Monsoon driven sea, smashes itself

into sheets of spray. On the land side, the battlements are high and massive, and from their summit there are lovely views in all directions, either towards the tumbling sea, or into the enclosure of the fortress, which, with its offices and churches, is like a little town. Across the harbour stretches a palm-fringed coast with blue mountains beyond, where Adam's Peak rises above its neighbours. The embrasures, the ordnance, the bastions, the lichen-grown magazines, speak of an age that is gone, and of hopes and fears and might-have-beens. Upon them all, Time has cast the mantle of romance.

. . . . .

228. Twenty-six miles further east, there is another Dutch fort at Matara, with the Rest House inside it facing the sea through a vanished rampart. In fact, only one side of the fort survives, though just across the Nilwala Ganga River the Redoute Van Eck (1765), now called 'Star fort,' is well preserved, and makes a charming residence for the P.W.D. Officer. Matara was originally a health resort for Galle: but it was also an important centre for the trade in spices. It is still an attractive little place, but the sea is treacherous, and one is warned against bathing. Throughout the coasts of Ceylon, the tides are so exceedingly small that they are almost unnoticeable: but the steady and long-sustained

Monsoon winds set up tremendous currents, and those at Matara are as dangerous as any I know. Their influence can easily be observed by the erratic behaviour of the waves.

229. Dondra Head, the southernmost point in Ceylon, is only an easy four-mile walk from Matara, eastward along the coast road. Here, as again at Adam's Peak, one is oppressed by the sense of limitless waters that spread unbroken to the south polar regions. Perhaps it is considerations like this that have intrigued men from an early date. Tennent says[1] "The headland has been the resort of pilgrims from the most remote age. Ptolemy describes it as Dagana 'sacred to the moon,' and the Buddhists constructed there one of their earliest dagobas, the restoration of which was the care of successive sovereigns. But the most important temple was a shrine which in very early times had been erected by the Hindus in honour of Vishnu. It was in the height of its splendour, when, in 1587, the place was devastated in the course of the marauding expedition by which De Souza d'Arronches sought to create a diversion, during the siege of Colombo by Raja Sinha. The historians of the period record that at that time Dondra was the most renowned place of pilgrimage in Ceylon; Adam's Peak scarcely

[1] Tennent's *Ceylon*, Vol. II, page 113.

excepted. The temple, they say, was so vast, that from the sea it had the appearance of a city. The Pagoda was raised on vaulted arches, richly decorated, and roofed with plates of gilded copper. De Souza entered the gates without resistance : and his soldiers tore down the statues, which were more than a thousand in number. The temple and its buildings were overthrown, its arches and its colonnades were demolished, and its gates and towers levelled with the ground. The plunder was immense."

230. The ruins of this temple of Dewinuwera, lie beside the modern village of Dondra, just where the Lighthouse road turns off. One handsomely carved gate survives, and before it and behind it, are rows of pillars which appear to have formed part of the approach to the temple. A stone basin, decorated with a design of twisted petals, remains ; besides two trellised windows (now incorporated in another building) ; and four fragments of a balustrade. These last, are decorated with the mythical beast called *Gaja-Sinha* (Elephant-lion) of which I imagine these are the oldest examples in the Island. They occur also in a pavilion before the 'Tooth Temple' at Kandy, and again on the monumental stairs at Yapahuwa. Unlike the dragon *Makara*, these creatures appear to be ascending the steps, but look back down them. Their trunks (much elongated) are curled

to form the sweep of the balustrade. Several 'Moon Stones' are lying about, but they are small and quite plain. In the walls, drains, and steps of the modern village, fragments of pillars can still be seen. There were, and still are, two places in Ceylon of superlative holiness in the eyes of Hindus, Trincomalee and Dondra, and the magnificent temples at both sites were wilfully destroyed by the Portuguese.

231. The celebrated Dondra Head Lighthouse stands at the end of the promontory, a mile away. Enormous green rollers fall with sullen monotony upon the rock-bound coast: for by the end of May the Indian Ocean, under the influence of the monsoon, has settled down into a continuous swell.

232. Here, in the most unlikely place imaginable, amongst the spray-drenched rocks, I caught in my hat a female of that rare butterfly *Elymnias hypermnestra undularis*. Its interest does not lie in its rarity, nor in its unexpected haunt, nor even in the fact that it is a mimic of *Danais plexippus*. The really significant thing about it is that it occurs in Upper India and in Ceylon, but *not in Southern India*: so that it may be included with the 'Himalayan type' of birds, as an additional link in the evidence of a land bridge with India. Incidentally, this specimen was a freak, having four white marginal dots on one hind-wing, and three very much enlarged ones on the other.

## CHAPTER XII

### PROVINCE UVA

(A Land of Tea and Rubber)

233. The lowlands are generally hot in April and May—but in 1927 the monsoon was early and erratic. Unusual rain tempered the breezes, and the climate was never oppressive. Still, these months are best spent in the highlands : and a wonderful network of roads lures one to them. Ceylon lends itself to travel. There are attractive Rest Houses in almost every place of importance. Concerning them, more information will be found in Appendix II.

234. It is a good thing to have a definite object in view, lest travel should become an aimless wandering, instead of being, as it should, a voyage of discovery. Is this not a platitude too often disregarded ? In the East, travel comes automatically to most of us, as a normal part of our duties or our recreations. How many people set before themselves any sort of study wherewith to gladden the journey ? And at the end, when we pass in review a more or less accidental experience in many lands, regret must surely arise at the opportunities that were lost.

235. Personally, I am the sport of fate : pitched

bewilderingly from country to country without much initiative of my own. The sale of three cars, and the break up of half a dozen establishments all within three years, has reduced me to comparative fatalism.

> " An exile from home, splendour dazzles in vain,
> Oh ! give me my lowly thatched cottage again ;
> The birds singing gaily that came at my call,
> Give me them with the peace of mind, dearer than all ! "

The most confirmed wanderer will yearn at last for these simple joys : but at least, while we are pilgrims, we should travel intelligently. For is not Travel the greatest of all educations, and is not education that which only ceases with life itself ?

236. In Burma my interests have been mainly ethnological, in Borneo geographical, in Malaya zoological, in England acutely financial, and now in Ceylon, whither I was sent in quest of health, the field of archæology is of such unique interest that I have not dared to pass it by. It is no small strain to adapt oneself rapidly to such varied calls, and to set it all down in orderly manner in a quick succession of books. Yet, the effort is necessary to certain dispositions. Literature is an exacting Mistress, a wayward and illusive Love, who offers rewards that are always just beyond reach. Perhaps some day, should that ' Little Grey Home ' ever materialize, I shall sit down with a pipe and think over all these glorious

and wonderful experiences, that hitherto I have hardly had leisure to ponder.

237. Ah, the butterfly trails of Southern Asia! Gleaming wings have lured me from land to land. But for us here, they are a mere pretext, a delightful excuse, for wandering abroad across the plains, and into the heart of the blue hills of Haldumulla.

238. The first stage is to Ratnapura, 56 miles from Colombo. For a while the road passes through squalid suburbs, but after that, the countryside is clean and lovely, with a tropical luxuriance of areca palms[1] and coco-nuts, that recalls memories of Malaya. Here, also, are the same shrubs and trees—hybiscus, lime, papiya, plaintain,[2] and golden bamboo: besides the angsana, rain-tree, jak[3], traveller's tree,[4] and casuarina. Even the same weeds occur, including *gloriosa superba*, the orange-flowered *Lantana*, and the sensitive plant. In short, we have in Ceylon most of that 'Cosmopolitan *flora*' that springs up all over Southern Asia as soon as the virgin jungle has been removed. It is partly cultivated by man, but partly it is introduced by obscure and accidental agents. Across these rich plains of rice, rubber, and coco-nut, it is a garden all the way: and the brilliant Kingfishers and Bulbuls, the Crow-pheasants, and the jaunty little magpie-

[1] *Areca catechu* and *triandra*. [2] *Musa sapientum*.
[3] *Artocarpus integrifolia*. [4] *Ravenala*.

COCO-NUT

A country-side, clean and lovely, with a tropical wealth of areca palms and coco-nut.

*Facing page 150*

robins, are no strangers to those who have travelled through equatorial Asia.

239. At intervals little towns are passed, whose outlandish names it is a duty to avoid. I feel inclined to apologize for the unfortunate names of the Kings, Pagodas, and Places of Ceylon—names which are not even always pronounced as they are spelt. The Tamil and Sinhalese languages lack 'zip,' and have, I believe, contributed no single word to the speech of the world, with the exception of *Mullagatawny*. The European reader naturally resents place-names like *Kellolupuliyaukulam*, forgetting that to the native it is probably as intelligible as 'Puddleton-on-sea.' But this does not exonerate the Author from blame, though I protest that, since these names are the only ones available, it is not possible to avoid them altogether. All that can be done is to use them sparingly.

240. As a matter of fact, the meaning of Sinhalese place-names are often rather attractive. The old name for Kandy was *Nuwara*. *Eliya* is a 'reflection,' or 'shadow.' So the new hill station is called Nuwara Eliya—'The Reflection of Kandy.' Of the common terminations *Gala* means a rock: *Wella* a field or plain: and *Mulla* the foot, or base, of a mountain

241. If one may judge of a country's wealth and activity by its motor-buses (and it is usually safe to do so), Ceylon is very much alive. Buses are parked

in every township and ply overloaded along all the roads where they are justly and bitterly cursed by motorists.

242. Ratnapura is slightly superior in size to some of the other places on our route. Its elevation is only 70 feet, but already we have approached the foot-hills. The town is surrounded by low ranges, and though they are of no great height, they are bold and picturesque in outline; and behind them rise the higher mountains, culminating in the sharp points and frowning walls of Adam's Peak. In the evening these uplands are usually hidden in clouds, and there is often a little thunder.

243. The 27 miles of country to Balangoda is largely devoted to the cultivation of rubber. But the orderly tea bushes also make an appearance. The palm trees of this low country are quite overrun by gigantic snails, and I believe they do much damage to fruit and vegetables. The elongated shells alone are often three inches long. These snails may be seen in scores ascending the stems of betel trees. The eggs are laid in the ground. Several varieties of large tree-climbing snails occur, and some are fairly local in their distribution. At Kandy, a round-shelled kind is common.

244. It is another motor drive of 27 miles to Haldum-mulla, through exquisite scenery. Hitherto we have

only skirted the high hills, but now the road definitely ascends the mountain sides. On one hand there lies a tangle of low ranges ; on the other rise bold and beautiful slopes of grass and gneiss, culminating in rugged peaks. Patches of jungle lie across the hills with green turf-lands between : while in the steep little valleys rice is cultivated on terraces. Here and there a small white pagoda occupies some romantic situation, but pagodas are not nearly so numerous as in Burma.

245. In the midst of such scenery lies Belihuloya, where a new Rest House has lately been established beside a torrent. Above it rise beautiful and imposing peaks—ribbed with stone, embattled with cliff and precipice, laced with falling waters, half veiled by passing mist, but always essentially green. The streams that come from the crags leap down in numerous cascades, and then flow brawling over stony beds, where dainty Wagtails sport on the wet boulders.

246. It was desirable for my purpose to travel by slow stages across the low country, watching the gradual change in the 'productions' with the rise in altitude. Perhaps it would have been pleasanter to come straight to Belihuloya, and to enjoy for some days the beautiful scenery of this district. But, experience of the tropical plains, not to

mention the fatigue of foot-slogging after butterflies during the hottest hours of the day, enables one to appreciate all the better the cool and fresh beauty of the mountains when at last they are reached. There is a valley near Haldummulla called 'West Hapulate,' which would compare with many in Kashmir. Steep grassy slopes rise from the lower end of this valley, but the mountains at its head are clothed with magnificent forest. A waterfall leaps down one side over cliffs of dark granulite, pouring in cascades of foam not less than 250 feet high, and plunging into a clump of trees that grows at the foot of the falls. The glen is filled with the melody of rushing waters. A cool, delicious breeze blows across the grassy mountains. Over all, is God's own sunshine.

247. And before I left it, I saw this lovely valley in yet another mood almost more arresting, when a storm spread along the crags, casting a strange lurid light over the precipices, and throwing into weird contrast the various shades of green—the fresh green of the grassy slopes, the emerald of rice fields, and the sombre jade of primeval forests.

248. Several interesting birds occur in these parts. One is evidently allied to the Pied Bush Chat. The black-backed Robin (*Thamnobia fulicata*), which is common in nearly all parts of the Island, is blue-black with a conspicuous chestnut vent, and a touch

of white on the wings in flight. It is particularly fond of playing on stones or rock. The Minivet is red with black head and wings ; but his consorts, at least in April, are less golden-yellow than in Burma. Most charming of all, is the White-browed Fan-tailed Flycatcher (*Rhipidura aureola compressirostris*), which is so friendly that you may approach to within a few feet of it. The under parts (except the throat) are white : the white eyebrows join in front, and nearly meet behind, leaving a black cap on the crown of the head. The tail is flirted in characteristic fashion, and is then white at the edges.

249. Haldummulla has an elevation of 3380 feet. The two-roomed Rest House (which is also the local club) stands out upon a spur overlooking the foot-hills. After rain, the plains can be seen far below like a blue-grey sea. A more delightful situation it would be hard to find. By day the air is fresh ; and at night, when one has looked out upon the Southern Cross, it is pleasant to pull on a blanket in bed.

250. The hills above rise to over 5300 feet, and it is a stiff climb to their summit by way of Batgoda Estate. The tea bushes, which grow upon most surprisingly stony ground, have been pushed right up to the crest line. The leaves from the top of this garden are packed in sacks weighing about forty pounds, fastened to a wheel, and then slid down a wire

of immense length. It takes a bag just forty seconds to shoot from the top of the mountain to the bottom.

251. At the crest of the range a surprise awaited me. I had expected to look down the reverse slope upon domes of foliage, as one certainly would do in Burma or Malaya. Instead, it was all open country. There is, in fact, no backing of virgin forest to the hills of Haldummulla. The scene that lay before me was very beautiful. A few red rhododendron grew along the mountain crest, and the grass was spangled with gay little flowers, including a yellow ground-orchid. Close at my feet, I was surprised to find Idalgashinna Station, and the railway line that runs to Haputale. To east and west the range rose in bold peaks. Below me, the ground fell away in long slopes of tea garden, and below that again in rice terraces : and then rose in a sea of bare, undulating hills, culminating in high mountains again about thirty miles distant. And in all that wide landscape, there did not seem to be a single tree ! Such are the ' patanas,' or grass-lands, and they recall the rolling uplands of the Shan States.

252. Below the Rest House at Haldummulla there is a brook that leads into the heart of a glade : and in that duskiness, gleam the green and blue wings of most exquisite dragon-flies. In the open lands beyond, occur many beautiful butterflies. That pest, the Spotted Locust (*Aularches miliaris*), is plentiful—

the body richly banded with black and red. It is particularly destructive to the Dadap trees, that are grown in Tea Gardens for the sake of their leaf manure.

253. This bit of country (below Haldummulla Rest House) has rather a park-like appearance. Its beauty and freshness, the dainty flowers on the grass, the great mountains above, are very impressive. Is it truly for the monuments of dead dynasties, and the ruin of their triumphs and wickedness, that Ceylon is famous: or even for the industries and products of our own restless age? I know not what I expected to find—but this I found upon the grass-lands of Haldummulla—Peace, and the Silence of open spaces and green hills: Silence that is compounded of the hum of insects, the chirp of birds, the sigh of breeze and water. And I found the Stillness that is made of sailing clouds, trembling shadows, and the movements of fearless creatures close at hand, when you have sat a long day-dream on the turf. For these things—all unconsciously—I have yearned, as the beasts by instinct crave they know not what, but are drawn thereunto. And like the beasts, I found in my day-dream that which I sought—the comfort, the solitude, the self-communion, the fresh loveliness of Nature, when the stillness and silence surge, enfold, obliterate. In that ecstasy arises a oneness with the trees and flowers, an understanding with the butterflies whose gorgeous

wings I came to steal, a brotherhood even with the poor green snake who crept forth to share with me the noonday shade.

254. Ah! the lessons that we fail to learn—the meaninglessness of desire, the folly of disputes, the emptiness of achievement. Hot lust for things that turn to rust and bitterness: and blindness for the things that really are worth while.

## CHAPTER XIII

## CEYLON HIGHLANDS

255. Haputale is one of the most convenient centres for touring the Highlands of Ceylon. In one direction lies Diyatalawa the old Boer Camp, now a favourite training ground for the troops. Bandarawela is only a few miles beyond. In another direction there is all the glorious country of Horton Plain; and in a third the Diyaluma Falls with the butterfly-haunted woods of Wellawaya below.

256. The Diyaluma Falls, that pour over a frowning precipice two miles from Koslanda, are one of the sights of Ceylon. According to the inscription on an adjacent rock, the actual drop of water is 570 feet, and the head of the Falls is 628 feet above the little bridge from which it is viewed. But these figures give only a faint conception of the majestic appearance of these falling waters, which are so awe-inspiring that it is hard to take one's eyes from them. The cliff itself is black granulite, and of immense height. A river leaps from its brow, the white festoons of spray into which it is soon dissolved, contrasting strongly with the darkness of the rock. I hardly know whether the Fall is most beautiful in bright sunshine, or when

the shadows of passing clouds cast a sinister light upon it. It is at any rate magnificent in every mood ; for first it descends in a sheer cataract until broken half-way down by a shoulder of rock that rises aggressively to meet it. In this encounter the water is smashed into spray, so that it completes its descent in eddies of mist that are blown this way and that by the breeze. Normally it plunges straight, but the wind may drift it far away, or may spread it across the face of the cliff like a gossamer veil. You can fix upon any festoon of water and see it drawn away and dissipated into rainbow. But if it should be so far blown out of its course as to miss the half-way buttress, then the water falls the whole 570 feet like a column of smoke that is dashed to pieces on the rocks below. It would be interesting to see it in a high wind when it blows even across the road. This superb picture of falling water is framed by the dark foliage of trees. There is something forbidding, and yet irresistibly attractive, in such stern aspects of Nature. The rock buttress rises up in bold challenge to the water, and indeed breaks it in irretrievable ruin ; but century by century the unwearing torrent has ground these granite walls beneath its heel.

257. *Diya*, in the name of these falls, is an archaic term for "water," and occurs frequently in place-names. According to some, *luma* may mean

"FALLING MIST"

The Diyaluma Falls leap 570 feet from the brow of a cliff, and are dashed into sheets of spray.

*Facing page 160*

"mist." The general idea seems to suggest "Falling Mists."

. . . . .

258. From Haputale the beautiful highland known as Horton Plain is easily reached. A fifty-minute train journey takes one to Ohiya (5820 feet). The railway line here follows close under the crest of the mountains, tunnelling through spurs, and traversing steep alpine slopes. The alignment is really quite a fine engineering feat. The hills are bold and treeless, and one looks out over grassy uplands that spread for miles and miles to the distant high ranges. There are little patches of jungle (the retreat of Sambhur) in the ravines and hollows, but the prevailing aspect is of bare, grassy slopes, dappled with sunshine and shadow.

259. It is a doubtful point whether these wide, open spaces, or 'Patanas,' were always as treeless as they are now. The former cultivation of coffee may partly account for deforestation; and the natives' disastrous habit of clearing ground for only temporary use has been practised in Ceylon as in other neighbouring countries. Of course, the destruction of virgin forest is followed by the disappearance of all rich humus. Then the soil goes too, till nothing is left but bare rock; and the rain-water, instead of sinking into the ground, rushes off. The occurrence

of frequent granite faces, and of cascades dashing down them, show that this process is already far advanced here.

260. To correct these conditions, extensive projects for afforestation are on foot. Vast areas have been planted with quick-growing eucalyptus and acacia, with the object both of protecting the soil and of supplying fuel for the population and for the railway. But already the railway is finding it cheaper to burn coal. Electricity may be the ultimate solution of a fuel problem, which is bound to become acute. Certain it is, that these mountains of Ceylon have been dangerously denuded in the past; and old residents will say that the climate is hotter now than it used to be. For all these reasons, no fresh land above 5000 feet has been leased or sold by Government for the last twenty years.

261. From Ohiya one walks along the railway track for half a mile to the first tunnel, and from there a short cut ascends steeply for a thousand feet. The appearance of raspberry, wild violets, forget-me-nots and hill-bamboo (*B. Vulgaris*), denotes the quick rise in altitude; and presently there begin thick forests of tree-rhododendron, with gnarled and twisted branches bearded with moss. An occasional head of scarlet bloom is seen against the background of white clouds.

HORTON PLAIN

Horton Plain is a grassy upland with an altitude of nearly 7000 feet. Trout fishing opens in May.

*Facing page 162*

262. At the top of this climb is Horton Plain, a grassy highland that in Kashmir would be called a '*Murg*.' It has been described as a plateau, and that is what it is—a breezy plain at nearly 7000 feet, but so undulating that it resolves itself into winding turf valleys, upon whose shoulders grow thick copses of stunted juniper and rhododendron. This dark foliage contrasts handsomely with the lighter green of the open meadows, whose grass is short and scattered over with dainty buttercups. The shallow valley bottoms are boggy, their rills eventually uniting in a black and peaty trout stream that winds across the plain below the Rest House, and which is regularly fished after the 1st May. Beyond this rolling country are seen the tops of neighbouring mountains. Beside the burn, one might imagine one was lunching on some Scottish moor: and to heighten the illusion, mists blow over in the afternoon, for frequent rain is the 'Entertainment Tax' that Nature levies in the East for so much greenery. The butterflies of these highlands are very interesting, and some occur nowhere else in the world. Such rareties are *Lethe daretis* and *Vanessa pyrameis nubicola*. A further note about them will be found in Appendix III.

. . . . .

263. From Ohiya the train climbs on to 'Summit Tunnel' at 6228 feet, and thence descends through

beautiful scenery to Pattipola—a most attractive spot. Little alpine valleys, hedged about by woods of juniper and rhododendron, are not unlike those of Horton Plain. The same sort of peaty streams occurs also at the next station, Ambawela, whose name means 'Boggy Field.' The line frequently crosses deep ravines, with little torrents and cascades dashing along amidst the rocks far below; while the great mountains lift their wooded spurs boldly into the blue sky. From these enchanted highlands one descends to Nanu-Oya, the junction of the branch line to Nuwara Eliya. At many of the stations there are fine bushes of *Datura suaveolens*, a shrub from which white, and rather coarse, trumpet-shaped flowers hang down, often in great profusion.

264. From Nanu-Oya an absurd little train pants and puffs up the steep incline to Nuwara Eliya. This portion of the journey is rather disappointing. Much of it lies through monotonous tea gardens, and nearly all the route already described offers far finer scenery. Nuwara Eliya itself, however, is charming. The open grass-land is scattered over with trees, houses and pretty gardens. There is a little lake, and a race-course. The winding roads are most attractive; and round about rise quiet hill-tops, culminating in Mt. Pedro, 8296 feet. Pedro, or to give it its correct name Piduru-talagala, is the highest peak in Ceylon.

NUWARA ELIYA

In the roads and gardens of Nuwara Eliya the trees are judiciously grouped in clumps of eucalyptus and fir.

*Facing page 164*

265. Some way out there are Botanical Gardens at Hakgala, and the town itself possesses a pretty park with trees judiciously grouped in clumps of acacia and eucalyptus, and of fir. The association of these two kinds of dark foliage in groups is a feature too of many of the roads, and there are frequent finely shaded avenues. The 'firs' referred to are really Casuarina and *Capressus macrocarpa*, as well as the Japanese *Pinus densiflora*, the Californian *Pinus insignis*, and the cedar—*Cryptomeria Japonica*. And all about the lawns are gay beds of flowers—hydrangea, phlox and Michaelmas daisies; while the surrounding meadow-land is bright with scarlet rhododendron and a golden prickly broom. This last is not to be mistaken for the thornless Cape Broom (*Genista canariensis*) that grows in the garden. Nuwara Eliya is 6200 feet. It is the social centre of Ceylon; and in April the climate is simple perfect.

266. It would be difficult to give an adequate impression of the extent to which tea is here cultivated. Its low bushes cover whole mountains, where the indigenous *flora* has almost disappeared before its advance. At Talawakele, whose name means 'Place of Jungle,' not one single clump of forest has survived.

267. The monotony of 'planting' has been somewhat alleviated in these days. Roads and motor-cars have mitigated the loneliness of it. On the other

hand, so the Planter tells us, it is no longer possible to 'get rich quick, and clear out': and, of course, not all the estates are situated on main roads. Some are still isolated, and then, no doubt, life is very lonely.

268. The tea and rubber gardens have to obtain their labour from India, where a special commissioner is posted to recruit. Tamils come over to Ceylon in thousands. There are agents to look after them, and indeed the Government of India's solicitude for these hordes of noisy immigrants is a standing cause of alarm and despondency, since the contract is a very one-sided affair. Besides giving a good wage (50 cents a day), the owners of gardens have to supply free quarters, rice and medicines. The sea passages of the coolies must be paid for both ways, and they may not be dismissed without notice. The labourers, on the other hand, are under no such obligations. They can quit without any notice at all. It is an almost universal custom of theirs' to demand an advance of pay on joining, yet it is too costly to enforce repayments if the men choose to leave without refunding. The contract indeed is hardly fair, and, like other measures, is apt to give the impression that the Englishman no longer receives bare justice. No one asks for preference, but equality of treatment would not seem unreasonable for the Victors of the Great

War. The British Lion is slow to wrath: and the World forgets that "*Ce petit animal est méchant. Quand on l'attaque, il se défend.*"

269. Nevertheless, by tact and industry, the plantations are made to thrive. Whereas the value of tea exported from Ceylon in 1873 was Rs 58, the exports for 1924 were worth Rs 215,000,000. Not only do tea bushes cover whole districts, but the acreage is always increasing: and the same applies also to rubber and coco-nut. In 1889 Ceylon exported 11 cwt. of rubber. In 1925 the value of the export was nearly Rs 170,000,000. Over four hundred thousand acres of rubber trees are now cultivated.

270. Tea and rubber began in quite a humble way about the time that the coffee plantations were destroyed by disease in 1875. They eventually saved the country from ruin in that memorable crisis.

271. It must not be imagined from what has been said here that no forests exist in Ceylon. As we have already seen, the flat Northern Plain, and indeed the greater part of the Island, is still buried in jungle. People are occasionally lost in it—and that is an extremely unpleasant experience. Not long ago an unfortunate planter lost his bearings, wandered for four days, and was eventually tracked to where he had died within a few hundred yards of a road which, had he known of it, would have saved his life.

## CHAPTER XIV

## ADAM'S PEAK

272. Many localities in India are sacred equally to Hindus and Mahommedans. Adam's Peak has the distinction of being holy to Buddhists as well: and indeed it seems to have arrested the attention of all sorts and conditions of men since a remote age. Its elevation is only 7360 feet, yet it is better known than scores of higher mountains. In fact, its reputation is world-wide. In this romantic pinnacle the land rises up grandly in one last gesture of challenge to the sea—but it is the last. If you look south from Adam's Peak, you are facing ocean that has no limit—at least no limit short of the ice walls of the polar seas. A suggestion of mystery has belonged to it from the beginning of Time, and was felt by generations of whom now we know scarcely anything. It rises from a knot of highlands whose very name *Malaya* is archaic. Tennent[1] translates this word as 'The region of mountains and torrents,' and the Malays, whose land is known to them as *Malayu*, believe that the word means 'mountains.'

273. The Sinhalese name for Adam's Peak is

[1] Tennent's *Ceylon*, Vol. I, page 375.

ADAM'S PEAK

The earliest legends of Asia are associated with Adam's Peak. It has been an object of pilgrimage since the remotest age. The lower picture shows the valley by which the approach is made.

*Facing page 168*

*Samanaliya* which, according to Forbes, is derived from Saman, or Lakshman, who accompanied Rama on his conquest of Ceylon. The red rhododendrons which cover the mountain are said to be specially dedicated to Lakshman.[1]

274. In the Mahommedan legend, of course, Adam is said to have fallen on the mountain on his expulsion from Paradise: and from this fact the Peak receives its most popular name, though the Mahommedan association is now the least important. Pilgrimages by Mussulmans seem to have been made at least since the 10th century.[2]

275. Early Christians, who were prepared to argue anything on principle, disputed the relative claims on Adam's Peak of St. Thomas and the Eunuch of Candace, Queen of Ethiopia—whoever she was.[3]

276. The Buddhist tradition, however, is probably the oldest. According to that, the Master alighted here on his farewell visit to Ceylon, and planted the impression of his foot upon the rock. Not only that, but all the four previous Buddhas in remote and mystic ages, came to this sacred spot, and left some mark of their passing. And so, from generation to generation, Adam's Peak has lured men up its cruel slopes: and in our own age pilgrims of all creeds

[1] Forbes' *Eleven Years Ceylon*, page 182–5.

[2] Tennent's *Ceylon*, Vol. I, page 603.

[3] Tennent's *Ceylon*, Vol. II, page 133.

and nationalities crowd thither in thousands. They are, however, chiefly Buddhists.

277. It may be said at once that there are no dangers at all in the ascent, at least from the Hatton side, where the climb is only one of 3600 feet. But from the valleys of Ratnapura, the ascent is almost from sea-level, and is much more severe. Along that route there are chains for people to catch on to, and these chains appear to be of very great antiquity. They are mentioned by the Mahommedan traveller Ibn Batuta in the 10th century; but no legend even suggests who put them there; and so well have they been fixed that, to this day, there seems to be no necessity for keeping them in repair. They are fastened merely at their upper ends, and the only accident of which I have ever heard is when some pilgrims, who were holding a chain, were blown over a cliff in a high wind.

278. There are no such perils in the ascent from Hatton, though the journey, like all meritorious acts, may be troublesome unless proper arrangements are made. But the difficulties have been duly exaggerated by those who derive profit out of travellers. A primus stove, hot coffee and bovril, are all very nice; but they unnecessarily complicate the journey. The plain fact is that, without any forethought, I made the ascent from Talawakele and back easily in a day.

From the railway at Hatton there is a twelve-mile motor drive to Maskeliya, and from there another four-mile drive through the tea gardens of Dalhousie Estate. Then the climb begins,, and though I am only a normally strong walker, I reached the summit in two and a half hours, and descended in an hour and three-quarters. Still, the climb is trying on account of its uncompromising steepness: and for the pilgrims, many of whom are old men and frail women, it is a serious business. Personally, I hold with them the belief that, if you went up Adam's Peak in seven consecutive years, you would be dead certain of attaining Nirvana.

279. The most popular way of making the ascent is at night by torchlight, the idea being to arrive at the summit in time to see the sunrise. At that hour the mountain throws an extraordinary pyramidal shadow across the country. Probably this is the pleasantest and easiest way: but numbers of people go up by day too, and so did I: and I think the scenery is better appreciated then.

280. When approached from the direction of Hatton, Adam's Peak is hidden for some time by intervening ranges. When at last it comes into view, it is seen to be a sharp, tooth-shaped peak, rising majestically above its neighbours. From every aspect on this side, it maintains this tooth-shaped appearance.

The summit is more or less bare, but the base of the tooth is wooded with juniper and rhododendron, and when these forests are reached the real climb begins—and it can only be described as heartbreaking. Indeed, I believe that cases of heart failure are not uncommon amongst the pilgrims. Within the last twenty years, the path has been stepped with granite almost all the way ; but these stairs are so steep, and so continuous, that the legs soon refuse to rise to them. The descent, when the knees tremble and threaten to give way altogether, is even worse. However, this part of the climb is at least well shaded, and when at last the trees thin away, the air is wonderfully refreshing. Already the surrounding mountains are looked down upon.

281. But still the cruel steps climb up : and gasping men and women sustain their courage with a continual flow of pious ejaculations. Perspiring clerks, and their exhausted wives, fortified with fans and pillows, struggle up in short spurts. An ancient nun, crying *Thadu Thadu*, battles bravely on. Many of these pilgrims are fulfilling some vow, made during an illness or other crisis, that if they, or their friends, are cured, they will climb Adam's Peak so many times. A jeweller from Colombo, subduing for the moment his shark-like instincts, becomes friendly without ulterior financial motives. The ardour of the climb,

and the benevolent spirit it induces, joins all classes for a while in one sweating brotherhood.

282. But *still* the steps lead up and up—steeper and steeper—till at last one is cheered by the clang of the bell which is being triumphantly rung by those who have already reached the top.

283. The summit has been built up into a small platform. It does not seem that the existing buildings are of any great age: though according to the *Rajavali*, the hero king, Prakrama Bahu, who made the ascent on foot during the 12th century, "caused a temple to be erected on the summit."[1] The holy 'foot-print' is of little interest, unless, of course, one wished to argue from it the existence of cement and concrete 500 years B.C. No exciting butterflies were met with during the ascent: and the only birds seen were at the extreme summit—a tit, and a bluish thrush with bright yellow beak and feet. It rather reminded me of the blue, yellow-beaked *Merula seebohmi* seen on the top of Mt. Kinabalu in Borneo.

284. The view from the summit is perfectly glorious. It was one of those lovely but fitful days, when vast clouds rise into the air, and mists are blown across the mountains. For a moment, Adam's Peak was enveloped in eddies of fog which melted away locally, permitting glimpses of upland and valley,

[1] Tennent's *Ceylon*, Vol. II, page 134.

until, relenting, the cloud rose like a curtain, revealing the whole landscape in all its loveliness. Various places in the country below were pointed out by a Buddhist priest who, after we had made friends, gave me a delicious cup of hot tea.

285. And so at length, regretfully, we descended again: and looking back from the foot of the mountain, wondered how we had ever reached that aloof and pointed summit. The last view I had of Adam's Peak was in the late afternoon, and it was then enveloped in a mass of flaming clouds. As I sat back in the car, and smoked the pipe of achievement, the thought came to me—"Thank God, that is over."

PERADENIYA

The Botanical Gardens are famous for their avenues of Royal Palm, Cabbage Palm and Palmyra. The last is here shown.

*Facing page 174*

## CHAPTER XV

### PERADENIYA

#### A Garden Forest

286. A railway journey of a few hours transports us from the true highlands to the lower hills of Kandy. Peradeniya, which is only 1576 feet, is the junction of the Haputale line with that which runs direct from Colombo to Kandy, and is famous for its beautiful scenery. Had we come straight from Colombo, the train would have traversed plains of rice and coco-nut such as those with which we are already familiar: and from Polgahawela would have climbed up into the hills, creeping along steep slopes, and across the face of precipices. This is the section beloved of tourists. The country is seen to best advantage from the railway, which takes a higher alignment than the motor road.

287. Peradeniya, of course, is famous for its Royal Botanical Gardens, which are second in beauty only to Kew Gardens—though the two are naturally so different that they can hardly be compared. Peradeniya is a garden, a park and a forest all in one: and its mature splendour is the fruit of over a century's affectionate labour. It goes back to the era of our

early struggles for supremacy, when the Dutch were successful rivals, at least in the Malay Archipelago. Experiments with far-eastern plants and trees, both here and in Penang, resulted from that jealous economic policy of Holland, that finally expelled us from the mysterious Spice Islands. Much of the *flora* of Ceylon, which we now take for granted, was introduced during our battle with Dutch 'monopoly.' What romance may not have brought about the planting at Peradeñiya of the Amboyna 'Cajuput Oil Tree'? The very name of Amboyna recalls a tragedy, and the ruin of British adventure in the Far East.

288. All who have lived in tropical countries must have regretted their inability to name so many familiar plants. Here, in Peradeniya, there is an educational feast, for the trees are admirably grouped and labelled, especially those three confusing families, the bamboos, palms and cactus.

289. The variety of tall bamboos that grow in clumps is very great, though few people differentiate between them. The greatest of them all, the Giant Bamboo (*Dendrocalamus giganteus*), is not really indigenous to Ceylon, but was introduced from Malaya in 1856. The clump of *Bambusa nigra* is almost as large, but the individual stems are slighter. Both are clean-stalked bamboos: but *D. strictus* has

PERADENIYA

The *Talipot* (left) is the greatest of all palms. It flowers (as here shown) once in its life, and then dies. Note the stilt-like roots of the *Pandanus* (right).

*Facing page 176*

whip-like branches issuing from the joints. It has also a more overarching habit, and the clump itself is so thick and close that one could hardly poke a stick in amongst its tight-packed stems. Of the much slighter and more feathery kinds, known usually as 'Hill Bamboos,' the commonest is *Bambusa vulgaris*. The Japanese form, *B. nana*, is rather more bushy.

290. The palms ordinarily cultivated in native gardens are the coco-nut, *Areca catechu* and *A. triandra*. *Crytostachys lakka*, the red-stemmed palm, is commoner in the Malay Peninsula than here. It is there known as *Pinang Raja*—'King Palm.' But the greatest of them all is the well-known Talipot Palm (*Corypha umbraculifera*) whose enormous leaves are used as umbrellas, for thatching, and for the manufacture of 'palm-leaf books.' These noble trees flower only once, at the age of about fifty years, and then die. Most of the specimens in Peradeniya were flowering in 1927.

291. There are three great palm avenues in these gardens, namely, those of Palmyra, Cabbage Palm and Royal Palm. The Palmyra (*Borassus flabellifer*) is distinguished by its rounded head, and by the stumps of dead petioles all up the trunk. The other two have tall clean stems—the Cabbage Palm (*Oreodoxa oleracea* having an open, feathery head : and the Royal Palm (*O. regia*) being inclined to thicken half-way up.

They are, however, closely related ; and if anything the Cabbage Palm is the handsomer of the two, by reason of its lofty and graceful carriage.

292. The cacti are a most confusing family. *Cereus grandiflora* rises in tall columns, with no secondary growths. A much larger species of the same type, here represented by a specimen forty feet high, is *C. peruvianus*. Both have lovely white blossoms which, however, only show their delicate beauty to the moon and to the night-flying moths. *Opuntia monocantha dillenii* is the common cactus with fat, prickly, pear-shaped leaves : and *Euphorbia antiguorum* has a more intricate, branching and tree-like growth.

293. There are all sorts of queer and freakish trees in this garden, whose flowers, leaves or roots are quaint and unusual. The Jak, of course, has its fruit growing from the trunk. The Cannon-ball Tree (*Couroupita guianensis*) produces all its flowers low down on stick-like branches. The *Pandaneae* are palm-like trees, whose roots resemble stilts. The greatest of them is *Pandanus leram*. Many forest trees which grow in crowded ground, or where the roots cannot expand freely, have to support their weight by throwing out buttresses above ground. The buttresses are often very thin, but several feet in height. Their winding growths form quite a

maze several yards in extent at the base of trees like *Ficus elastica.*

294. It is, however, the more common *flora* that the student will be glad to recognize and identify—the familiar shrubs and trees which, for most of us, grow nameless in our midst. Such are the Traveller's Tree (*Ravenala*), the common Plantain (*Musa sapientum*), and the Jak (*Artocarpus integrifolia*). The beautiful Gold Mohur (*Poinciana regia*) is really a native of Madagascar. In almost every Ceylon garden is seen a dainty coral-pink creeper, which in Burma is known as *Taik Pan.* Its scientific name is *Antignon guatemalensis,* which suggests that even this most common plant, now widespread throughout the East, is not really indigenous. It belongs to that 'Cosmopolitan *flora*' that spreads itself in Southern Asia wherever the virgin jungle has been removed.

295. In every forest there is seen a shrub whose upper leaves are dead white. The little flowers are orange, and are much resorted to by certain butterflies. This is *Mussaenda frondosa.* In *M. erythrophylla* the upper leaves are red.

296. Most of the common tree-parasites, so characteristic of tropical jungles, are represented in the 'Liana-Drive,' but it is disappointing to find that they are not labelled. One of the huge, woody creepers, whose ponderous loops are seen also in Burma and

the Malay Peninsula, is *Plecospermum Spinosum.* Another giant creeper, whose flat, ribbon-like stem is dented, rather like the links of a chain, is really a Bauhinia-*anguina.*

297. The calling and whistling of birds at Peradeniya in the dawn is very remarkable. When the shadows are still long, and the lawns are wet with dew, a thousand restless creatures awake to renewed activity—the oriole, the bulbul, the shama. The Ceylonese Loriquet (*Loriculus indicus*) flies in cheerful parties into the bloom-laden trees, to scatter blossoms recklessly upon the grass. The blue-tailed Indian Pitta (*Pitta brachyura*) lurks in the copses. Most attractive of all is *Tersephone paradisi paradisi*—the Paradise Flycatcher. It is common too at Anuradhapura, and other places on the Northern Plain. In April it has not yet assumed its splendid breeding plumage. By May the tail has grown to a great length, but the general colouring is still chestnut. Presumably it turns white a little later, as in Burma.

KANDY

Kandy, one of the most attractive places in Ceylon, nestles around a charming lake.

THE TEMPLE OF THE TOOTH

The Tooth of Buddha, brought to Ceylon in A.D. 311, was captured by the Portuguese in A.D. 1560, and destroyed by them. The present "Tooth" was produced by King Wimala Dharma some years later.

*Facing page* 180

## CHAPTER XVI

### KANDY

298. Kandy is perhaps the most charming of all the Ceylon hill stations. It nestles round a lake that lies amidst low, wooded hills. The banks of the lake are well shaded, and glimpses of an island are frequently obtained through a tracery of branches. It is hard to say whether Kandy lake is most enchanting in the dancing sunshine or when it sleeps placidly beneath the moon. It is, however, always fascinating.

299. The site of the Lake was originally a paddy plain belonging to the palace, and it was only in 1812 that one of the Kings of Kandy captured the waters by building the present embankments. The beauty of Kandy is its chief attraction. Its other interests are somewhat forced. The 'Buddha Relic' is spurious; and the 'Tooth Temple' which enshrines it, is neither old nor particularly beautiful, though it is 'snapped' and gaped at by hordes of uncomprehending tourists. Some time ago, in London, I saw a film of the 'Life of Buddha.' It was excellent so far as it went, but the grand and impressive story was told by a Hindu hotel tout on one of his cadging expeditions, to a vacuous English girl who was trying to look

intelligent between the purchase of a false ebony elephant and a brass cobra from Manchester. The setting of that film always recurs to me whenever I cross tourist routes in the East. The historical hotch-potch served up by so-called 'guides' to American Globe-trotters, and by them presumably noted down in countless diaries, must be a substantial contribution to the world's fiction. At Peradeniya the science of botany is expounded at a price (a stiff price) by the Rest House 'Boys' after meal hours.

300. Still, the 'Tooth Temple,' or Dalada Maligawa, is not without interest. It is an object of the greatest veneration to the Sinhalese, and it is the direct descendant of a long line of temples in which the real tooth was housed in Ceylon up to the time of its destruction. Its stone pillars and wooden superstructure are derived from ancient indigenous types of architecture, and are therefore interesting to anyone who has already studied the ruins of Anuradhapura. The octagonal tower was added by the last King of Kandy in 1810, and from its balcony he was accustomed to look down on gorgeous pageants of elephants when the 'Tooth' was shown to the people. The adjacent Audience Hall (A.D. 1783) is, however, of greater interest. With a stroke of genius, the British Government converted it into the Supreme Court of Justice. So, instead of standing empty and

desolate, like the Royal Palace in Mandalay, it continues to represent Law and Authority in the eyes of the natives. Kandyan Chiefs are seen attending it in those picturesque robes and head-dresses that one imagined only survived in old book-plates.

301. It was to Kandy that I retired again at the end of my travels, to rest, think and write. The atmosphere of this, the last of the Sinhalese capitals, was naturally in harmony with my present train of thought. Several charming paths wind through the wooded hills. Lady MacCarthy's Road and Lady Horton's Road are the haunts of many lovely butterflies: and seats have been placed in situations commanding the finest views. Here you may watch the high white clouds that ride into the sky. Cool breezes sigh across the forest trees; and the Kandyan Hills, blue, green and red, lie dappled with sunshine and shadow. It is the sort of landscape that draws one away out of oneself all unconsciously, so that, while the eyes linger upon those restful uplands, the spirit follows all sorts of pleasant and romantic trails into the land of day dreams.

## CHAPTER XVII

## TRINCO

302. On leaving Kandy, we quitted the Ceylonese Highlands with their grass-lands and tea gardens, and descended to the great Northern Plain to visit the several ancient sites that have already been described in Book I. Apart from its historic associations, Matale, at the foot of the Kandyan Hills, is an immaculate little town of very considerable beauty. It has always been the seat of important Kandyan Chiefs. It possesses a really charming garden, where the scent of flowers hangs heavy on the evening air; and its lawns and open spaces are wonderfully green. There is at least one thing for which I envy the inhabitants—their cemetery. It is really an extension of the Saxton Gardens, where the dead rest in peace under their flaming Angsana and Gold Mohur,—with a lovely mountain panorama on all sides. There at least (though probably not before) an Urban District Councillor of Matalé, having passionately pleaded his cause (free of costs) in the highest of all Courts, may hope for that tranquillity that is denied him by his colleagues on this imperfectly reformed earth.

303. At Dambulla, and generally throughout the

Northern Plain, the water is bad and hardly fit to drink. The climate is hot and malarious, though in April mosquitoes are not yet numerous. The soil is very gritty, and one's feet soon get sore with walking; and a pair of boots is torn to bits in no time. The forests are free from leeches. Their place is taken by a jungle tick which bites secretly, but leaves a most painful and irritable wound.

304. Villages are fairly numerous—a point worth noting, because in the highlands (except of course round Kandy) the scarcity of villages had been a continual surprise to me. There, small towns are frequently met: and collections of wayside huts occur that owe their existence to the roads. On the tea and rubber estates there are coolie lines—barracks in which a considerable part of the population is housed. The greater part of the hill populace is thus divorced from the land, and is as ignorant as town dwellers are of all that concerns the forests. Jungle produce, such as a bit of cane or bamboo, is only procurable in a shop, and has probably come from Colombo, if not Rangoon. All this is very surprising. In Burma, Malaya or Borneo, a wandering Naturalist can be sure that the little boys will have an intimate acquaintance with the habits of wild animals. In the Ceylon highlands the most little boys know of wild animals is what Shelley wrote in his 'Ode to a Lark.'

In the countries I have mentioned, a judicious distribution of coppers will instantly produce insects by the handful, and in Borneo I made extensive collections of beetles, phasmudae and spiders in this way, once the news was well spread ahead that a lunatic was coming. But in Ceylon no such thing is possible amongst an estate-bred and semi-commercialized Tamil population. The occurrence of villages now on the plain was therefore all the more welcome.

305. The long drives to Sigiriya and Polonnaruwa through dense, unending jungles, are very beautiful. The forest trees are not tall. I should say their average height is less than 30 feet : but the undergrowth is thick and matted. Enormous iguana are occasionally seen ; and on one occasion, while motoring, we ran past a herd of Spotted Deer.

306. Towards Anuradhapura, the forest is varied now and then by attractive hills, by little patches of cultivation, and by lakes and swamps full of lotus. This same kind of country continues all the way to Trincomalee, though the lakes are larger and more frequent. That at Kantalai is a large body of water. Here the climate is damper, and flowers become plentiful. Beside the more conspicuous flowering bushes, there is an extraordinary wealth of tiny blooms amongst small plants in the grass. They are really worth stopping to observe—all these unconsidered

white and yellow stars, blue bird's-eye and dainty florets of red and coral pink. Presently you come to palms and the sea.

. . . . .

307. I suppose everyone in the world has heard of Trincomalee. It belongs to the era of sea-romance along with Amboyna and Bencoolen : but I wonder if it conveys any mind-picture to those who have not actually seen it. With Malacca, Tavoy and Moulmein, it shares a glory of long ago, when the great ports of to-day were mere fishing villages. They are a tale that is told—these ports of an ancient fame. They are sunk in poverty and decrepitude, but they have their proud legend. Without ambition, without regret, they sleep now beneath their venerable trees, in the shadow of their frowning forts and batteries. Restless modern enterprise is but a smoke smudge on the horizon. Such are Malacca, Tavoy and Moulmein : and such (still) is Trincomalee—a hazy historical tradition.

308. As a matter of fact, the history of Trincomalee will hardly bear looking into. It has been singularly inglorious. The Portuguese showed no interest in the place whatever until 1622, when their position in Ceylon was already seriously threatened by the Dutch. The fortress they hurriedly built at Ostenburg was quarried from an ancient Tamil monument, 'The

Temple of a Thousand Columns' which stood upon the promontory, and which the Portuguese ruthlessly destroyed. Finally, as we have seen, the Dutch took the place, but abandoned it without a blow to the French in 1672. The latter, however, were forced to evacuate for want of supplies: and the present Fortress was built by the Dutch in 1676. In 1782 it was occupied by a British force from Madras, but the French surprised it, and the British were ignominiously taken home whence they came. At the end of the war Trincomalee was restored to the Dutch, and remained with them till 1795, when they surrendered Ceylon, with hardly a struggle, to the English. The history of Trincomalee, a place of great strategic strength, has therefore been one of unrelieved disasters—the reason being of course that Portugal and Holland, each in their turn, were conquered in Europe. Portugal was eaten up by Spain; the Netherlands succumbed to Napoleon; and these catastrophes at home naturally paralysed colonial enterprises abroad.

309. Geography is one of the most important elements in history: and natural features dictate to destinies of Man. Trincomalee is one of the outstanding exceptions to this law. The magnificent harbour, which has few rivals in the world, has never been used for trade, nor, as we have seen, have its

tactical features ever resisted attack. Colombo, a far inferior port, which has only been rendered safe for ships by a lavish expenditure of treasure, has taken its place on the trade route, and is destined to hold it. Singapore is another key position that was only recognized late in time (A.D. 1819), and almost accidentally. But once the genius of Raffles had lit upon it, its advantages were obvious. As he himself said: "It is worth continents of Territory." Colombo owes its present grandeur to the most paltry causes. "Its selection," says Tennent, "was determined solely by its proximity to the only district in Ceylon which produced the precious cinnamon—and for years after British occupation the conquerors were influenced by the same motives as their predecessors."

. . . . .

310. Trinco reminds one rather of Malacca, though it is neither so large, nor so picturesque. But it is similarly roofed with red tiles, and the houses are antique and solid, embellished with stone gates and porches, deep verandahs and tall pillars, after the style of a more generous age, when people lived in the East like gentlemen. The 'Old' Rest House, which claims to have been a Dutch office, has walls so strong that it is almost impossible to drive a nail into them. It still contains Dutch chests and cabinets, much treasured by their Burgher possessor. The

Catholic Church (1752) is a practical building, with deep verandahs and a low, tiled roof. The interior is dark and inviting: and the door stands wide open; while that of the Protestant Church in the fort is generally locked. The roads of the town are neat with the tidiness of maturity, and are shaded with beautiful rain-trees. At corners there are banyans, supported on clumps of roots, and casting grateful pools of shade. Angsana, gold-mohur and acacia rain their gracious petals on the streets. The *neem*, *zibin* and *Tanaung-bin* of Burma flourish here also, and the tamarind casts a restless tracery of shadows on the ground.

311. Trincomalee consists of an Inner Harbour—that which is renowned for its depth and security—and an outer coast. The two bays of the outer coast are separated from each other by a promontory on which stands Fort Frederick. Each of these bays in itself is an important roadstead, and on the neck of land that divides them from the Inner Harbour lies the town. The entrance to the Inner Harbour is some miles to the south.

312. Fort Frederick was built in 1676: and as we have already mentioned, it is of Dutch origin, and occupies the point of a promontory. Massive walls protect it on three sides. The fourth side—that towards the sea—is already sufficiently guarded by

Nature; for the cliffs are high and precipitous, and a swell beats ceaselessly along their feet. Swamy Rock, one of the finest of these precipices, has been an object of Hindu pilgrimage for centuries, and as we have noted, the site was originally occupied by the 'Temple of a Thousand Columns' till the Portuguese destroyed it in 1622, and from its material built the first works on the site now known as Fort Ostenburg.[1] To-day Fort Frederick fulfils the peaceful duties of housing the offices of the Irrigation Department. Its ancient guns are used as posts, or for anchoring the flagstaff: and its cannon balls, once nicely arranged in little piles along the roads, are now scattered over the ground like derelict pills. The casements, where formerly guns frowned from the heights, are now screened with cactus and the sweet-scented mimosa. I have always had a friendly sentiment for these useless old forts of the Indian Ocean since the days—ah! so long ago—when, as a boy, I used to play in Fort William, and tricycle on the cement roof of an old barrack. A Commander-in-Chief lent me that roof: and there was a dear old Adjutant-General who solemnly reprimanded me for firing my air-gun near an East India Company's magazine.

313. There is a lovely view over the bays from the

[1] Knox's *History of Ceylon*, Chap. XLVII, page 274.

cliffs of Fort Frederick, and towards the Inner Harbour. A mile away a school of porpoises frolic in the shining sea. The air is so still that you can hear the 'flop' of their falling after every leap. A small stone column on the brow of the cliff marks the spot where Francina Van Reede, the daughter of a Dutch official, threw herself over in 1689, while the ship that bore away her faithless lover was passing out of the harbour. The inscription is now wholly obliterated, and few who pass that way know the tragedy of poor little Francina.

314. In the Monsoon the bay below the fort is dangerous for swimming on account of the currents which sweep round it: but, without venturing too far, we had some delicious early-morning bathes from the sandy beach. The bathing near the reef by the Fort is perhaps better. The water is clear and limpid, and the friendly little waves, which break off short with a playful slap, are straight from the mighty deep. It seems that the sea must sink suddenly to a very great depth, for fish can be seen quite close in to the shore. I watched one fellow fleeing with frantic leaps from a young shark. The shark was clearly visible, travelling at lightning speed along a rising wave. The impression I retain is of a transparent green wave, high and tottering, and of the shark streaking down the length of it at an in-

credible rate, while the wave was in the very act of breaking.

315. On this same beach I was interested to see a 'water boatman' cast up by the waves. I seem to have heard or read of these insects being found in the ocean, but I had never before seen one there myself.

. . . . .

316. The Inner Harbour—how shall I describe the beauty and grandeur of it? It is like a lake, for no open sea is visible. The low, wooded hills fold it to their bosom.

317. They say the whole British Fleet might lie there secure amongst the hills, and that the *Renown*, when she put in with the Prince of Wales, was quite lost in that wide and incomparable harbour. It has been suggested that its extraordinary depth, even close to the shore, is due to volcanic action. But the harbour is empty, except for those queer old hulks whose white wings have almost disappeared from the high seas, and which lie and die in Moulmein, Malacca, and Trinco, and nowhere else in the world. Their jibs and spankers (if such be their correct names) are set in the morning sunshine—but not for sailing. It is merely a caretaker's drying after the rain. Coasting vessels put in occasionally; but, speaking generally, no ships avail themselves of these safe waters.

The harbour is abandoned to the hulks and the *catamarangs.* You may hire one of the latter and go out after mullet, but it is not very exciting. The views thus obtained of creeks and islands are more interesting: and after the sun has set, if there are high, bright clouds, they sometimes reflect a strange bronze lustre on the wavelets.

318. Away on the hills lie the bastions and batteries of Fort Ostenburg, which once commanded the entrance of the main harbour. Their massive ruins lie overwhelmed by the jungle, and walls that were designed to resist powder and shot have succumbed to the fig tree, which treats them with as little respect as it treats the monuments of Dutthagamini and Prakrama. And no one will release them from that fatal grip—at least not for a millennium, and until the British and Dutch have become a picturesque legend. An old wooden door still hangs on its hinges, beside which, no doubt, sentries stood for decades, looking at nothing after the manner of sentries. Cactus and neem have grown up in the roofless barracks where soldiers dressed their cots—the ancient sort of soldiers, now seen in military museums, eager to tell all who will charitably listen, about "When I was in Trinco in '81." A stone inscription (comparatively modern) marks the place where Gunner Redstone landed in 1888 after being blown from a

gun on the battery above, during the salute of minute guns fired for the Emperor Frederick. A miserable way of dying—and for a German Emperor too—and a dead one at that !

. . . . .

319. But while Trinco sleeps beneath its rain-trees, the old world had swung the full circle. The Indian Ocean, once the key of the Far East, has achieved the new status of a British lake. Slowly, without design, the process has been effected, and is now an accomplished fact, though the British themselves are hardly aware of it. From the Cape to the Red Sea, Aden and the Persian Gulf, round by India, Ceylon, Burma, Malaya, and down to Australia lies an unbroken arc of British territory and British influence. And this British lake commands, in an undisputable way, all western entrances to that ocean of future destiny—the Pacific. In Trincomalee, the Sleeper Wakes.

. . . . .

320. Rip Van Winkle in his long sleep—stirs. Is he about to rise ? Trincomalee, in spite of its age, is assuming a new energy. Signs of prosperity are not wanting. The roads are neat and trim. Since the 2nd May (1927), the whistle of a daily train has been heard : a Welfare Clinic opens its doors on Thursdays : and a Sailors' Home looks yearningly

for sailors. There is a sign-board marked "Balasubramaniam: The Trained Councillor." It does not say what sort of counsel the gentleman gives—but probably on any subject you like. A notice, flapping on the wall, reads "Vote for Abdul Rassol: The Man of the Times." Here at least is a definite opportunity of saving the Empire. Trinco stirs: but one has an uneasy feeling that sacrilegious people might lay violent hands upon it, cut down its ancient trees, and disturb the mimosa upon the crumbling emplacements. After all, in a place like this, antiquity is an asset: and one would regret to see any more of the proud old guns ignominiously turned upside down and chained together for railings. One would resent to have the scattered cannon balls arranged in little wayside pyramids, and dressed by the right. The vandal who made any such hostile gesture would be a disturber of the Peace. But who shall say if one day —pray God not in our day—Trincomalee, which belongs to the dead age of Faulkland and Juan Fernandez, will not step forth into Europe's morning paper head-lines: and people at home, so sketchy in their knowledge of the Empire, will look up T. in the Index of *The Times* Atlas.

. . . . .

132. From the condemned dockyards, issues the ghost of an old man. At least, his appearance is frail,

and he is dressed in white drill : but as I watch, he shouts a business-like command :

" Get a move on, lads."

I look at the lads—two naked Tamil coolies, struggling with a hand-cart—and *they are moving.*

## CHAPTER XVIII

### JAFFNA

322. The peninsula of Jaffna at the extreme north of Ceylon is, geologically speaking, a recent formation produced by a gradual uplift of coral beds upon which have accumulated the sandy material swept down from India by ocean currents. It is a flat plain only some eight or ten feet above sea-level, and its lower parts, which have not yet risen from the sea, form shallow lagoons either along the coast or spreading inland. Though connected with the ocean, these lagoons are, for some reason, only slightly brackish: and as they are continuous across the southern end of the peninsula, except for the artificial railway embankment, it would really be correct to regard Jaffna as an island. However, these waterways are so shallow that formerly they were habitually forded by elephants and other animals from the mainland of Ceylon. Their favourite passage, by which they raided the ripe palmyra palms of Jaffna, is still known as 'Elephant Pass.' It is a featureless place, and suffers a strong wind from April to August, but the old Dutch fort beside the lagoon has been converted into a pleasant rest house: and Elephant Pass is a convenient retreat from Jaffna.

323. The Jaffna promontory, low and sandy though it is, is covered by millions of coco-nut and palmyra palms. Both are graceful trees, but such a continuous richness is monotonous. A certain amount of rice is grown, and the light soil is particularly suitable for the cultivation of tobacco. Jaffna, indeed, is an important agricultural district, which the skill and energy of the Tamil has turned into a veritable garden. Tamils have been in occupation for hundreds of years, and have to be regarded now as indigenous. There is literally not a Sinhalese left in this part of the island.

324. The Jaffna district is traversed by a network of roads ; and along the railway frequent stations and sidings bespeak a large and pushing population. But the charms of Jaffna town are not what one might be led to expect from the enthusiastic accounts that have been written of it. There is too strong an element of dust and Tamil. Tamils are not distinguished for their manners. They have the most childish habit of staring : and their ' yes ' is said with a negative shake of the head which very obviously means ' no.' For instance, when they said they wanted to go ' dry,' they really meant they didn't, as is shown by the marked increase in drinking. Malicious persons would have you believe that the constituents were tight when they voted, but I have it

on the best authority that that is only a vulgar jape. The practical effect of these reforms is that drink, even at the Rest House, is unobtainable unless you know where to get it. In addition to all these disabilities, the climate is hot and would be unbearable but for the wind. This wind, however, is not a friendly, refreshing breeze, but a howling, nerve-racking hurricane that moans through the houses, and sends dismal 'sand-devils' spinning down the streets. And after a tormenting day, spiteful gusts blow out one's lamps at night. The clean, open sea is shut off by an outer coast, and the shallow lagoons have a stagnant smell. Nevertheless, Jaffna has the reputation of being healthy.

325. Jaffna was forty years a stronghold of the Portuguese. The neighbourhood of Mannar was the site of St. Francis Xavier's missionary successes. Six hundred of his converts were, however, massacred by the Jaffna Raja. This persecution was punished by the Portuguese in 1544, but the outrage was again repeated. John III, says Tennent[1], then directed the Viceroy of India to take revenge. In 1560 Don Constantine fitted out another armament. The Bishop of Cochin, who accompanied the fleet, "erected an altar on the shore, and in the presence of the invading

[1] Baldaeus, in Churchill's *Voyages*, Vol. III, page 147. And Tennent's *Ceylon*, Vol. II, page 29.

army inaugurated the assault by celebrating mass. The attack was successful but costly ; many fidalgos were slain by the cannon of the enemy, the city was taken, the palace destroyed, and the king forced to come to terms.—Amongst the incidents of the victory, De Couto dwells on the seizure by the Viceroy, of the *Dalada*, the celebrated Tooth of Buddha, which had been carried to Jaffna for safety during commotions in the Buddhist (Sinhalese) states.—Subsequently, the King of Pegu (Bayin Naung) sent an embassy to Goa to tender as a ransom three or even four hundred thousand cruzadoes. The fidalgos were unanimous in their wish to accept this offer as a means of replenishing the exhausted treasury of India. But the Archbishop, Don Gaspar, was of a different mind. He firmly resisted the offer, as an encouragement to idolatry. Consequently, the tooth was placed in a mortar and reduced to powder and burned in the presence of the court. Its ashes were scattered over the sea.

326. The Portuguese were expelled by the Dutch in 1658, and it is the Dutch who have left the strongest impression on the architecture of Jaffna. Indeed, this influence is the only thing that makes the town interesting. The fort is really a remarkable place. It was built in 1680, four years after that at Trincomalee, and is constructed of coral rock

which has wonderfully withstood the ravages of time.

327. The Dutch Church stands inside the fort. It is a squat building in the plan of a Greek cross. According to J. P. Lewis[1], it is the oldest existing ecclesiastical Dutch monument in Ceylon. The date over the entrance is 1706, but older buildings must have occupied the site, since there are tombstones of 1666 and 1672 let into the floor, and which are apparently *in situ*.

328. The older Portuguese Church (I quote Mr. Lewis again) stood near the opposite corner of the fort green. Its bell, dated 1648, is preserved in the vestry of the Dutch Church, and bears the legend: *N. S. dos Milagres de Jafanapatao*, "Our Lady of Miracles of Jaffnapatam."

329. The interior of the Dutch Church looks enormous, the effect of space being heightened by its emptiness. The only furniture are some quaint old pulpits, and the Governor's state pew. Lewis says the original columns of this pew were twisted, but they have since been replaced by rounded ones with capitals.

330. Most remarkable of all, are the magnificent granite tombstones that have been let in as slabs into the floor. In many cases the carving is of a high

[1] J. P. Lewis' *Tombstones and Monuments in Ceylon*, page 215

order: and here, beneath their heraldry and their virtues, lie the old Dutch soldiers, governors, and merchant princes. There is something very impressive in their loneliness in the great empty church they built. Amongst the very few English graves is that of Maria Wallett (1814) with the request: "And pray let her remains lay undisturbed."

331. The early European monuments of Ceylon have suffered many vicissitudes. At Jaffna, the Dutch broke up Portuguese tombstones, put the fragments into their mortars, and bombarded the Portuguese with these relics of their own dead.[1] The monument of the greatest of the Portuguese generals and administrators, Phillip de Oliveyra, once occupied that chapel of 'Our Lady of Miracles,' but it has now disappeared together with the church. It was probably disturbed when the Dutch repaired the fort, and built the existing church. The memorial at Mannar of the wife of a "Captain of Mannar" at the time of the Spanish Armada, survives, though it was used by early English officials as a pig and horse trough. In view of all this vandalism, the pathetic plea for Maria Wallett—"And pray let her remains lay undisturbed"—does not seem so very unreasonable. Lewis mentions another inscription on the ramparts

[1] J. P. Lewis' Introduction to *Tombstones and Monuments in Ceylon*.

of the fort at Kalutara (near Colombo) which he suspects as being addressed to some future Public Works Officer—" Respect and spare the remains of our lost child."

332. As a result of all these and other depredations, only about sixteen Portuguese stone inscriptions survive. One of these, a large boulder now in the Gordon Gardens at Colombo, is clearly dated 1501—that is, four years earlier than the arrival of d'Almeida. It is supposed to have been the work of Portuguese captives or adventurers of whom no other record survives. It is, however, not a hurried bit of work, but an elaborate composition.

333. Dutch monuments have also suffered considerably. After the cession of Ceylon, some were transported to Java and there lost. Others were used for building houses and drains. But according to Lewis, 225 Dutch inscriptions remain.

334. Amongst the curious buildings in the Jaffna Fort is the 'King's House,' formerly the quarters of the Governor, and now used as an official residence. The exterior is almost mean : but the astonishing spaciousness of the interior suggests happy days of the 'pagoda tree.' The surprising length and breadth of the verandah recalled memories of Metcalfe House in Delhi. The large and heavy furniture of that age was none too big for the apartments it had to fill.

The dining-room of 'King's House' is 43 feet square. The vast kitchen was evidently designed for the roasting of whole oxen. The Sessions Judge's eggs are now poached on a tiny oil stove in one corner. His little iron bed, in the centre of an immense floor, might be the subject for a Heath Robinson picture. One can imagine His Honor setting out at dawn on a route march to the tooth brush on a distant wash-hand stand.

## CHAPTER XIX

## THE TRIUMPH OF PURE REASON

335. Socrates taught (or if not he, it was President Wilson) that the human animal, left to himself, can determine his own salvation. The theory supposes that the wise men of the State, having been chosen and elected by a far-seeing and responsible body of voters, will direct their country, without discord or self-interest, through the shoaly waters of progress. Having formulated these axioms, their author, whether Socrates or Wilson, died : and left the world to make the best of them. The happy working of Democracy in Ceylon may be witnessed in the harmonious deliberations of the Matale Urban Council where, we were told during the resulting litigation, that the Chairman is nearly out of his mind. It is interesting to note that the Sinhalese Embassy to Rome in the reign of Claudius laid special stress on the fact that in those bad old days the Island was " Free from the evils of judicial strife."[1]

336. He would be a bold man who claimed to understand the Spirit of Democracy, as interpreted by a section of the Oriental World. The essence of

[1] Knox's *History of Ceylon*, page 4.

the doctrine seems to be a cantankerous temper, coupled with an insatiable passion for talk. It is only necessary for any sane suggestion to be made regarding, say, an Electric Installation, or a site for a University, to set politically minded persons frothing at the mouth. Every proposal is, on principle, worried into a controversy, which results either in loss of money, or in a horrid waste of time. For once an opinion is formed, no argument on earth will move its originator from it, though it is usually about a subject which does not concern him in the least, or one upon which he is abysmally ignorant. The truth is, that half-educated people know everything : only the wise appreciate their own limitations. A mere veneer of civilization, alas, will not correct the persistence of queer and twisted workings in a savage's mind. A too sudden freedom from age-long tyranny may only produce an exaggerated sense of wrong, where originally wrongs were safest endured in silence. Those who are but newly emancipated from the crushing oppression of their own kind, are the most apt to have advanced ideas about self-determination, and the rights and equality of man : and while raving at the assumed brutality of those who have really brought justice, may be blind to their own oppression of others. Nationalism in the East, of course, is purely a political stunt, to be exploited so long as no personal sacrifice is involved. In the schools students cannot be induced to study their own literature or history. With regard to the various financial contributions to the Empire, when Malaya is frequently giving us a million or so, Ceylon, on the contrary, 'collects but does not subscribe.'

. . . . .

337. Unfortunately, Freedom and Democracy are not synonymous. There was a real freedom for individuals under the benevolent and lenient system that was condemned as 'Bureaucratic.' Fatherly kindness (and the people miss it sadly now) has no place in reformed constitutions, whose guts are made of red tape. But these are things that the world has to learn for itself. Meanwhile, independence is easily interpreted as the right to be churlish, where the maxim has never been heard that 'Manners Maketh Man.'

338. The fact is, that human progress is not a matter of proclamation. It follows certain inexorable laws. The world is improving right enough, but you can neither hurry it nor retard it. The pace is based on Cause and Effect, and any attempt to meddle with that, is doomed to failure. You can force a vote upon a man ; but if his real instinct is to stick skewers into his back, or needles through his tongue, or to walk on fire, or roll round and round the temple of

his faith, his mind will be set on those things. He is apt to overlook the higher aspects of democracy. And the Legislative Councillors to whom he entrusts the destinies of his country, will be the kind who will busy themselves about opposing the tarring of roads, since tar is very disagreeable to voters who roll on roads. There are, however, or there should be, bigger problems to worry about.

. . . . .

339. It is characteristic of British Governments to be ideal pioneers, but to fail just when the civilization they have planted and fostered begins to demand freedom and the refinements—that is at the critical point where paternal, autocratic rule ends, and democratic government begins. Their fault sometimes lies in giving too little, but usually in giving too much. As far as can be observed, and in spite of a certain amount of bickering, the turn seems to have been safely taken in Ceylon. The people are, at any rate, free now to manage their own affairs if they can. Unfortunately, the late Mr. Montagu was an ostrich who buried his head to certain axioms—that houses should not be built on sand, and again, that houses divided against themselves have a habit of falling. All that is hereditary and traditional may be disregarded, the wise men of old may be called fools and dolts by superficial visionaries, but the Cosmic

Laws of Cause and Effect are, unfortunately, still Cosmic Laws. They may be ridiculed, but they still operate. However, Ceylon has now been in contact with Western civilization for over four hundred years —that is, since the advent of the Portuguese in 1505. It lies at the convergence of many sea routes. As the result of these influences, it follows that its inhabitants are not unduly conservative, but on the contrary are ready enough to accept fresh ideas. Education up to a certain standard is widespread, and English is spoken even in the most unexpected places. Not all who receive education, however, are capable of turning it to account. On many it is wasted. But the man who evolved the Power Scheme now before Government was a Sinhalese; and there is a high percentage of cultured people who have polished manners and a considerable aptitude for business. Too often, however, ambition is limited to the desire for posts in the Law, in Medicine or under Government.

340. On the other hand there are signs that Ceylon, even after four years, is already a little weary of all this *Furor loquendi*, and of the bauble of Democracy. Every legislator, whether in Council or Committee, having once stated his views, is anxious to get on with the work; and it is very annoying when colleagues insist also on expressing themselves at length. And if they are of a different religion, tradition and nation-

ality, it is only an extra aggravation if their talk is clever. Further, 'Power' looks such a desirable toy while it is in the hands of others: but it is apt to become an exacting nuisance if we have to administer it ourselves. In many quarters the opinion is growing that, after all, the old officials did not do the job badly, and that if they are foolish enough to take it on again for a ridiculously inadequate wage, there could be no harm in indulging them. Unfortunately, the official producing families in England have become so distrustful, that they are unlikely to turn back from the new fields of employment which have now begun to attract them elsewhere.

341. Ceylon is a Crown Colony. The Governor is 'assisted' by an Executive and a Legislative Council: and a Colonial Secretary is appointed by the Crown. The Legislative Council, which at present has complete financial powers and very little responsibility, was reconstituted in 1923 so as to consist of 12 official and 37 non-official members. All but 3 are elected on a communal or territorial basis. As matters now stand, the appointment of a Royal Commission has been announced to examine the situation: and it is generally supposed that some means will be devised for making the Legislative Council a more responsible body—that is, a body that is responsible for its actions. A rigid written Constitution, and the

creation of an independent Court of Appeal, are what people seem to expect : but the future is on the knees of the Gods. Leaving aside the question of ' Experience ' with which, it seems, we are prepared to dispense, it is obvious that any sort of self-government depends on two principles—Good Will and Responsibility.

342. Meanwhile, the better-class Sinhalese, and in fact the free-thinking communities of all races, whose interests are endangered by the delegation of power to a pack of noisy and quite irresponsible lawyers, are really getting apprehensive. There are " large and important minorities which might be rendered perfectly defenceless," and the anxiety of those with a serious stake in the country is probably voiced in the recent utterance of the Governor, Sir Hugh Clifford, when he said : " I do not believe any Constitution can be sound or satisfactory when it draws a sharp dividing line between power and responsibility—conferring Power on the Legislative Council and leaving the Executive Government to make such issue as it may with the decisions recorded even against its advice." As for the great, voiceless masses, in whose name, and on whose behalf, all this pother has (in theory) arisen, they are serenely indifferent. All *they* want is to be let alone.

343. In all moderate societies therefore—that is

amongst all classes who have anything to lose—there is a growing resentment at the quite unmerited prominence that the talkative politician has achieved. What the people want is peace, and the suppression of the agitator. Like the poor, bothered Dauphin of France they cry : "Oh, I wish he'd keep quiet, or go home."

## CHAPTER XX

## THE ETHNOLOGY OF CEYLON

344. Naturally, the ethnology of a small, isolated island cannot compare in interest with that of continental areas, particularly when its races are considerably mixed as they are in Ceylon. In a like area of 160 miles by 140, one could find, say in Burma, a score of different races represented, some of whom retain their purity to a remarkable degree. Still, the ethnology of Ceylon deserves more attention than it has received.

345. The census return of 1835, showed a population of 1,250,000. By 1857 it had increased to 1,700,000. The population to-day is about 4,300,000. and of this about 2 millions are Low Country Sinhalese, 1 million Kandyans or Hill Sinhalese, half a million Ceylon Tamils, half a million Indian Tamils, and one-third of a million Moors and Mahommedans. There are in addition 13 thousand Malays, 30 thousand Burghers and Eurasians, 8 thousand Europeans and 4½ thousand Veddas.

346. The fact that this population has been nearly quadrupled within a century, lends significance to the fact that Ceylon produces very little of her own food

supplies. This is partly due to the fact that other produce like tea, rubber, cocoa, and coco-nuts are more paying, and partly to the fact that foreign rice is more palatable, and therefore more popular. But a minor cause may be that, at least part of the existing rice land, is rented to the cultivator by the native owner at such an iniquitously high figure (sometimes 50 per cent of the profits), that there is hardly a living wage to be derived from this form of cultivation. When the growing population of Burma needs all its own rice, as those of Japan and Java already do, the question of food supplies is likely to become acute in countries like Ceylon and the Malay Peninsula which have hitherto had the advantage of devoting their entire energies to more profitable and spectacular production.

347. The Sinhalese, as we have seen, furnish nearly three-quarters of the total population. Their origin is still a matter for speculation, and is a problem for which no satisfactory solution has yet been found. They are undoubtedly a very ancient race. I am not entirely satisfied with the accepted theory of their Indian origin, though there is no reason to doubt the tradition of their landing in Ceylon from India. It is only recently that the Mongolian origin of the Malays has been recognized, and the Sinhalese seem to have many traits in common with them.

I would suggest that arguments such as I have advanced for Malays in my *Malaya* (pages 95 to 101) might perhaps be extended to the Sinhalese with modifications, bearing in mind Huxley's warning (*Man's place in Nature*, Chapter IV) that, in the realms of ethnology, language is a very uncertain guide. My own knowledge of the Sinhalese is quite superficial, but from what I have seen of them, their Indian origin is not convincing; and that opinion was formed before I read either Knox's mention of a tradition that Vijaya came from Tenasserim,[1] or the footnote on the subject—which I have not since been able to find—in Tennent's *Ceylon*. There is a certain lightness of limb, and slimness of waist, that is not Aryan. The evidence of hair in this case seems inconclusive. The face is often hairless, but the hair of the head has a waved tendency. From what I am told the Sinhalese are dignified, cruel, inconsistent, reckless, and passionate: and though it is doubtless undesirable to rely too far on racial characteristics, their similarity to those of the Malays and Burmese is at least suggestive.

348. The Sinhalese have the usual qualities of Buddhists who, by some irony of fate, often display a recklessness that is the reverse of what their calm religion teaches. Crime is on the increase, and, as

[1] Knox's *History of Ceylon*, page 16.

in Burma, it is largely crime with a knife—unpremediated crime, committed on the spur of the moment. A Sinhalese will, under provocation, kill a man without compunction—but a cobra he will never harm. There, the primitive Naga cult peeps out from beneath a superficial Buddhism. The rule against taking animal life is more strictly observed than in Burma.

349. There is an ancient feud between Lowland and Highland Sinhalese, which is as deep-seated as the hostility between Sinhalese and Tamils. In character the Plainsmen and Hillmen differ considerably. The lowlanders are said by some to be more reliable and amenable, while others claim for the Kandyans that they are natural gentlemen, and that courtesy and hospitality reside in the mountains.

350. As a race, the Sinhalese are quarrelsome—the usual cause of disputes being women and property. By their laws of inheritance, property is divided equally amongst the children, with the result that ultimately it is reduced to infinitesimal proportions. Sixty years ago Tennent mentions a case in the District Court of Galle relating to a disputed claim for the 2520th part of ten coco-nut trees, so it is not surprising that disputes are even more acrimonious to-day.

351. The Sinhalese are very careful about keeping

property, however small, in the family. They will pay up the mortgage for a relative, or even buy back his estate for him, in a very generous way. Fortunately, there is still unlimited waste land that can be taken up, so that economic pressure is not yet severe, though it has been noticed that the number of Sinhalese employed as labourers is increasing. This is considered a bad sign, since the people have a marked preference for working their own properties, rather than on the Estates. It is hoped that the opening up of land for 'small holdings' will ensure the continued independence of the cultivating classes, and there is such a scheme already on foot.

352. The Tamils have inhabited Ceylon for many hundred years, and those who are bred in the island have to be regarded separately from those who have merely come over in recent times to find a living. Labour immigrants tend to return again to the land of their birth. The Tamils are an uncouth, noisy people without that courtesy and refinement that is inbred in many Oriental races. They are lawyers to a man, and imbibe a taste for litigation with their mothers' milk. It is not a lovable quality. Between Tamils and Sinhalese there has naturally been some fusion : but, owing to their traditional animosity, it has not been as considerable as one might suppose.

353. Besides the Sinhalese and Tamils there are

several smaller groups, namely, Moors, Malays, Burghers, and British. Burghers are the descendants of early Dutch settlers, and are an important element. All Sinhalese with Portuguese names are not necessarily of European origin. Many are pure-blooded Sinhalese, whose ancestors adopted Christianity—perhaps temporarily at the time of forced conversions. Kandyans now usually take surnames from their village names: and amongst low-country Sinhalese there is a growing fashion of assuming the names of the great kings and queens of their history.

354. The Moors are of Malay, Arab or South Indian origin. They are mostly traders, and in Galle and Trincomalee are numerous. There is a considerable domiciled community of Malays, who are spoken of as quiet, industrious and reliable. Other Malays come over temporarily, but these do not bring their women.

355. Within recent years, the Veddah aborigines have almost disappeared. Originally they were forest nomads who lived by hunting, and they still occur in the Province of Uva, east of the mountains, and again north of Anuradhapura. But they have been so far absorbed, and have acquired so considerable a civilization that, except for a few communities, they are no longer easily recognizable.

356. The Tamils, of course, are Hindus, and as such

observe 'caste,' though not as strictly here as in India. But the survival of 'caste' amongst Sinhalese Buddhists is surprising, since Buddhism was largely directed against such distinctions. Its continuance may be attributed to the encouragement given to the system by Sinhalese kings—at least those later ones who were often of Tamil descent, and who sympathized equally with both religions. 'Caste' does in fact occur to a limited extent in other Buddhist countries like Burma, where hunters, grave-diggers and pagoda-slaves (often the descendants of war prisoners) are outside the pale of society.

357. In Ceylon, fishers and hunters (who, by the nature of their professions, take animal life) are similarly ostracized; and there is a 'caste' of musicians. Other outcasts are Mukkuvars, Waggai, Oddes, Kinnaras, Kuruvars and Ahikuntakayas. The last are gypsies. Even the despised Rodiyas, whose very name is derived from the Sinhalese word *rodu* meaning 'filth,' are not the lowest of these untouchables. There are grades of degradation even below them for barbers, bootmakers, and others. Offending nobles were pretty frequently degraded to the Rodiya class in former times, and the 'caste' received some degree of uplift from these aristocratic recruits. But under the Kandyan Kings, the Rodiyas were continually reminded of their abasement. They might

not cross a ferry, enter a village, till land, learn trades, or even worship in the pagodas. They could not build walled houses, but were forced to live in sheds: and neither the men nor the women were allowed to wear any sort of garment above the waist or below the knee. Under British administration the lot of these unhappy outcasts has much improved. A Commission enquired into the question of their betterment in 1904. The disabilities under which they lived have been removed, the Courts are open to them, and in the last two census reports they have not been separately enumerated. There are estimated to be only about 1500 Rodiyas in the island now: but naturally their redemption is not easy after so many centuries of contempt and oppression.

358. Modern conditions have tended to lessen 'caste' distinctions in the higher grades. The marriage customs, wherein money plays an important part, have helped to remove barriers by the alliance of blue-blooded but impoverished aristocracy with families less well-born but better endowed. 'Caste,' however, is still an important factor in the social life of Ceylon.

## CHAPTER XXI

## CONCLUSION

359. In Ceylon, the Past—the forgotten and disregarded Past—is imperturbable. Arrested in stone, it is a thing that has been, still is, and, without regard to the transient affairs of to-day and to-morrow, always will be. For centuries to come Anuradhapura will sleep in the shadows, and leaves will fall upon the granite steps of Mahintale. For millenniums the breeze will blow against Mahinda's Couch, breasting the plain : and Prakrama will gaze out upon the ruin of his proud handiwork. For æons and periods Adam's Peak and the Rock of Sigiriya will resist the monsoon rains. They are subject, like everything else to the Law of Buddha. *Aneiksa : Dhoka : Anatta*—'All things are subject to decay' : but, on the whole, Time has dealt leniently with Ancient Ceylon. Its monuments are uprooted and scattered, but what remain have acquired a quiet dignity : and so long as man exists he will be attracted to them by reason of their beauty, their boldness, and their venerable antiquity.

360. Man himself—at least Modern Man—is but an episode in the history of Ceylon. Tamil, Portu-

gese, Dutch—perhaps British too—they come and they go, with a clamour about spices, cinnamon, coffee, tea, rubber, or whatever is the latest money-making craze. Tyrannies pass imperceptibly into Democracies, and thence—less imperceptibly—into new Tyrannies. But still the wind rustles the leaves of the Bo Tree. As formerly, so now also, Man, frenzied with his greed or his piety, fails to learn the great Lesson, the clear Message, that came into the world two and a half millenniums ago beneath that very tree: "This only do I teach, oh Disciple: Sorrow and the Ceasing of Sorrow."

361 As formerly, so now, Men strive and fret for what they acknowledge to be futile. Yet, admitting it, they still strive generation by generation for that which is empty: for those things which moth and rust do corrupt. Generation by generation the things which men laud and praise with the lips, are neglected in the heart. So lust, and anger, and the needs of Man increase continually, and hatred breeds hatreds worse agian.

362. But still the Message comes to us clearly across the ages. The Past is fogged by legend, by the ignorance of Man, and by the futility of priests: yet through it all the Law remains—emphasized and repeated to Ananda by Buddha at his death: "This *only* do I teach: Sorrow and the Release from Sorrow."

By greed, lust, hatred and craving ye are bound to the Wheel of Bitterness. The eradication of these things from the heart is Freedom, Enlightenment, the Deliverance from Sorrow." That is the message of the Thuparama Dagoba, which it has testified to heedless generations from the days of Asoka down to our own: and that is why Humanity, frail and ignorant, blinded by its supposed needs and its hot desires, yet turns with instinctive reverence to the Teacher who spoke intimately and individually of a World Embracing Tenderness

363. "He is dead! He is dead!" cried Ananda, the 'Well Beloved Disciple,' as he stood anguished before the body of the Buddha. Ananda is represented thus in the rock-cut figures at Gal-wihara. But "Nay Brother," said another, "He is not Dead. He is Passed Away." And Ananda, rebuked in the first act of his ministration, took heart. The calm beauty of his understanding is preserved to us in that imperishable stone.

364. Something of all that is the esoteric meaning of Ancient Ceylon. It was a rough age of rough men. Bloody and cruel were their deeds sometimes, limited their understanding; but, such as they were, they laid hold of a Truth, and for a time at least strove, according to their lights, to live up to it. And they wrote it in books and upon rocks, that it might pass

down the centuries for the comfort of posterity. That is why we may look back to them with affection. Mahinda we may love for his gracious benevolence. Tissa we revere for his enthusiasm. Walagam Bahu, the rough soldier, caused the Buddhist legend to be written down, so that many nations have since consulted his work, and received inspiration. It was only a 'version,' already corrupted by four centuries of error: but in the Cave of Alu-wihara was recorded the Truth as it was then known to those comparatively savage men. How much more beautiful it must have been, clear and fresh from the Master's own lips! All we know now, is that it was a clarion call that roused from its apathy the whole civilized world. It was a sublime, eternal, fearless wisdom that weary humanity would do well to study again. We cannot suppose that the nations were electrified by the crude thing that Buddhism is to-day. Yet even now, in its mutilated form, one cannot discern any teachings which are not recognized to be wise and good.

365. Little comprehending, a little have I writ—stumbling with paltry words to express the spirit that inspired the age of Mahinda. Separated now by two thousand years from that period, we can only strive to read between the lines of extravagant legend, seeking to interpret the spirit of those times by the

few shattered monuments of brick and stone that have survived. Graceful gestures in granite speak of a spiritual elation ; and vast piles of senseless brick, representing the sweat and anguish of a generation, are yet expressions of dumb, half-formulated yearnings.

366. And the utter ruin to which all those proud monuments have been brought, makes them more eloquent now than ever they were in the days when they glittered with gold-leaf and gems. For are they not, in their decay, irrefutable evidence of the Truth—' In all things there is Impermanence ' ?

*Thadu*

# APPENDIX I

## ITINERARY

| 1927 | | | |
|---|---|---|---|
| March | | | |
| 24th | Colombo to Ratnapura. | 56 miles. By road. | 70 feet. Across the Plain. (Chapter XII.) |
| 27th | To Balangoda | 27 miles. By road. | 1700 feet. Approaching the hills. |
| 30th | To Haldummulla. | 27 miles. By road. | 3380 feet. Climbed definitely into the hills. |
| April | | | |
| 3rd. | To Haputale. | 7 miles. By road. | 4700 feet. (Chapter XIII.) |
| 4th | To Horton Plain and back. | Rail. 1 hour. Road. 1 hour. | Highland Plateau. 7000 feet. (Chapter XIII.) |
| 5th. | To Koslanda and back. | 32 miles. By road. | Diyaluma Falls. (Chapter XIII.) |
| 6th. | To Talawakele. | By rail. 3½ hours. | 3970 feet. |
| 7th. | To Nuwara Eliya and back. | By rail. 3 hours. | 6200 feet. (Chapter XIII.) |
| 8th. | Climbed Adam's Peak. | | 7360 feet. (Chapter XIV.) |
| 9th. | Talawakele to Peradeniya. | By rail. 5 hours. | 1576 feet. (Chapter XV.) |
| 13th. | To Kandy. | | (Chapter XVI.) |
| 14th. | To Matale. | By rail. 1 hour. | 1137 feet. |
| 15th. | To Alu-wihara and back. | 2 miles. By road. | Cave Temple. (Chapter VI.) |

1927

| April | | | |
|---|---|---|---|
| 16th. | To Dambulla. | 28 miles. By road. | A descent to the Northern Plains. 500 feet. (Chapter VI.) |
| 18th. | To Sigiriya. | 11 miles. By road. | Rock-fortress. (Chapter VI.) |
| 21st. | To Polonnaruwa. | 34 miles. By road. | Second Sinhalese Capital. (Chapter VII.) |
| 28th. | To Anuradhapura. | 62 miles. By road. | First Great Sinhalese Capital. (Chapters II to V.) |
| May | | | |
| 5th. | To Trincomalee. | 66 miles. By road. | (Chapter XVII.) |
| 8th. | To Maho. | By rail. 7 hours. | |
| 9th. | To Yapahuwa and back. | 4 miles each way. | Ruins. (Chapter VIII.) |
| 10/11th | To Jaffna. | By rail. 11 hours. | Dutch remains. (Chapter XVIII.) |
| 12th. | To Elephant Pass. | By rail. 2 hours. | (Chapter XVIII.) |
| 14th. | To Kurunegala. | By rail. 8 hours. | Short time capital. (Chapter VIII.) |
| 18th. | To Negombo. | By rail. 4 hours. | Dutch and Portuguese remains. (Chapter XI.) |
| 21st. | To Galle and Matara. | By rail. 6 hours. | Dutch and Portuguese remains. (Chapter XI.) |
| 22nd. | To Dondra Head and back. | 4 miles each way. | Ruins and Headland. (Chapter XI.) |

| | | | |
|---|---|---|---|
| 1927 May 25th. | To Kandy. | By rail. 13 hours. | To rest, think, and write. |
| June 3rd. | To Kadu-gannawa. | By rail. ½ hour. | |
| 5th. | To Polgaha-wela. | By rail. 1 hour. | |
| 7/9th. | Colombo. | | |

# APPENDIX II

## NOTES ON TRAVEL

367. Besides a railway guide, certain advertising publications, and a brief summary of routes in Murray's *India*, there is no comprehensive guide-book to Ceylon. It may, therefore, be useful to add a few notes on travel.

368. *Routes*. My own route is given in Appendix I. It was designed to cover as many beauty spots and places of archæological interest as possible, and it includes the best butterfly grounds. It passes from the South Coast, up through the knot of Central Highlands, and so down across the Northern Plains where lie most of the ancient ruins. There are, of course, endless variations by which the same objects could be achieved. A network of roads and railways traverses the country. The time occupied was two and a half months, allowing halts of three days at most of the places, and of a week at sites of special interest, such as the old capitals.

369. *Transport*. The ease and rapidity with which the

Island can be seen depends largely on the amount of money that it is proposed to spend. Ceylon is essentially a motoring country. The official charge for hired cars is supposed to be 50 cents a mile ; but since the return journey is *invariably* claimed, on the supposition that the car will go back empty, the actual rate, unless one is up to the ropes and prepared to haggle, is a rupee a mile. That, for many people, is prohibitive. There are 4000 miles of road ! The ideal, and the most economical way, to see Ceylon with comfort and freedom is to buy a cheap second-hand car, and sell it at the end for what it will fetch.

370. *Motor Buses.* Scores of motor buses ply along all the roads. They are not generally patronized by Europeans, but may be used in an emergency, or on special occasions. Mail buses, where they run, are satisfactory : but private buses have no other recommendation than cheapness. They have no fixed hours of starting, and if not sufficiently full may not start at all. A severer tax on one's patience than a Ceylonese motor bus, I cannot imagine.

371. *Rest Houses.* It is almost true to say that there are Rest Houses everywhere, except at Colombo, Galle, Kandy, Nuwara Eliya, Bandarawela and Anuradhapura, which are all big places with hotels. The *Hotel Suisse* in Kandy, where I rested at the end of my tour, gave me very reasonable terms, and I am glad of an opportunity of acknowledging it. The Rest House is an institution of which Ceylon is justly proud ; and the system that has planted them in every place of any importance represents a considerable organization. They meet all one's immediate needs, and are as clean as can reasonably be expected. Mosquito nets and other necessities are all supplied at a moderate price, but it is highly advisable to carry one's own sheets and pillows, and a cake of extra strong carbolic soap. Residence

is only permitted for a period of three days, but an extension is easily obtainable on application to the Chairman of the local Road Committee.

372. The tariff is moderate, and is in theory fixed : but in skilful Tamil hands it is capable of amazing variations according to the appearance of your face. Bills for precisely the same occupation and meals for the statuary three days range mysteriously from Rs 24 (a Sinhalese Butler) up to Rs 50 (a particularly rapacious Tamil). But not even the Tamil can compete with some of the European Hotels, which openly maintain two tariffs—one for strangers and one for residents. Always claim to be a resident ! Meals at the Rest Houses are as palatable as chickens and custard puddings can render them—but I made the strange discovery that a curry of half a dozen dishes, followed by fruit, is not only a much nicer meal, but is very much cheaper than the variations of chicken which are supposed to be a European's normal food.

373. *Baggage.* The less baggage you have, the better. In the big centres, the ordinary well-dressed society is met. In the country, 'shorts and shirt' is *de règle.* The plains may be hot : the hills are sometimes chilly. It is convenient to send a box of surplus clothes from point to point by rail.

374. *Children.* Rest House food lacks the nourishment required by growing children. Ideal milk, biscuits, malted cod-liver oil (or their equivalents) should be carried, together with suitable medicines. Good shops are rarely met with, except in the very biggest centres.

375. *Books.* The standard book is Tennent's *Ceylon.* It remains the most authoritative work. Cave's *Ruined Cities of Ceylon* is also informative. Scattered notes on Archæology and Natural History are contained respectively in the *Ceylon Journal of Science*, and *Spolia Zeylanica.* The

butterflies are described by Mr. Orminston in Vol. XI of *Spolia Zeylanica*. If staying in some big centre like Kandy, it is convenient to join the local library.

376. *Maps*. The Survey Department's folded *Motor Map of Ceylon* is excellent. Price Rs 3.95.

377. *Postage*. *Letters:* local and India 5 cents, abroad 9 cents. *Postcards:* local and India 3 cents, abroad 6 cents. There are post and telegraph offices at all places on my route, except Sigiriya and Polonnaruwa.

## APPENDIX III

### BUTTERFLIES OF CEYLON

378. At different altitudes, and in different situations, many kinds of climate are to be found in Ceylon. The north-east and south-west monsoons bring varied conditions to places, according as they are high or low, or are on exposed or sheltered slopes. There are localities with a yearly rainfall as low as 37 inches (as at Hambantota); and others, like Ratnapura, where it is well over 150 inches. Within a few hours you may sweat at the foot of a mountain, and shiver at its summit. It is therefore difficult to make any comprehensive statement either as to the climate, or as to the proper seasons at which butterflies should be sought: but generally speaking, those illusive insects are in greatest profusion in April and May before the heaviest rains have deluged the forest. Incidentally, there must *be* forests: and in a small island so highly cultivated as Ceylon, it is possible to go for a hundred miles without seeing the smallest patch of indigenous jungle. In Borneo and the Malay Peninsula, the best altitudes for butterflies are from 800 to 2000 feet.

The same is probably true of Ceylon, provided the selected area is well forested. The uplands of Haldummulla and Haputale possess species not found elsewhere, and are recommended by such a veteran collector as Mr. Orminston : but from my own experience, and from the almost total disappearance of the indigenous jungle, I should never expect any great profusion there at any season. These places, however, are certainly convenient centres from which to visit varied grounds, from Wellawaya at almost sea-level, to Horton Plain at 7000 feet. These highlands may therefore be recommended for hill species, and for certain rare butterflies that are 'peculiar' to the mountains. A considerable variety of types occur in the woods of Kandy (1600 feet), especially along the walks called Lady Horton's and Lady MacCarthy's Roads. In the low country, the best grounds I found were at Ratnapura (70 feet), and at Dambulla (500 feet) along the Kurunegala Road.

379. On the whole, the butterflies of Ceylon are disappointing. Uninstructed people, when they note millions of Pieridae in a flight, imagine they were seeing a lot of butterflies. Such a sight, of course, is always interesting, but a collector while collecting requires variety too : and the number of species seen in any one day is very small in Ceylon, as compared with Burma, Borneo, or the Malay Peninsula.

## PAPILIOS

380. The *Ornithoptera* are represented by *Darsius*—a magnificent black and yellow butterfly. The fore-wing is entirely black : and the splays that usually occur in this type, as in the Malayan *Ruficollis*, only show on the reverse. The golden-yellow 'plates' of the hind-wing have a fine

satin-like sheen, and the black border beyond is very deep. The neck and the sides of the body are red. The female is a good deal less common than the male, and keeps to the dense jungle where she hovers so high, and so close to the foliage, that she is quite difficult to take.

381. The largest butterfly in Ceylon is *Papilio memnon parinda*. The fore-wing in the male is black, with cobalt-blue splays across it, tapering away towards the apex. The hind-wing is blue, with a double row of bold black marginal spots. The female is similar but strongly washed with yellow, especially on the reverse. In the dry season these great butterflies are extremely shy and cautious, and have a maddening habit of dashing into a glade, and then not returning to it for twenty minutes. They are like restless gleams of silver-blue, that flit ghost-like through the jungle, where there is scarcely any hope of taking them. At all times they are given to flying through thick foliage: but in the rains they frequently come down to lantana, and other flowers ; and even visit gardens.

382. *Papilio crino* is another lovely but illusive butterfly. It is black, closely peppered over with green, and displays a bluish blaze on each wing. It is represented in the Malay Peninsula and Borneo by *P. palinurus :* but *Crino* is more shy and swift. The only successful way of catching it is to rush in upon it at once before it can dive into the undergrowth.

383. *Papilio Hector* is black, but with a lovely blue sheen. The fore-wing has thin white splays across it in two distinct groups : while the hind-wing is decorated with glorious crimson spots. The body, too, is nearly all crimson. He is more a lover of open country than any of the papilios hitherto mentioned ; but all of them, with the exception perhaps of *Crino*, have a marked liking for evening flights

at sunset, contrary to the custom of most butterflies, who do not move about much after their noontide rest. In the plains *Hector* is easy to take, and is even slothful : but in the mountains, where he is only an occasional visitor, he is shy and restless. Once alarmed, he goes off like a rocket, and you can watch him against white clouds, climbing up and up for half a mile into the sky. It is a very pretty sight.

384. The commonest of the papilios is *Polytes*, a 'Blue Beard' amongst butterflies. Of his three different wives, one resembles the male, another mimics *Papilio Aristolochae* so closely that it is not easy to find it, and the third (*Romulus*) mimics *Papilio Hector*. The significant point is that *Romulus* (the mimic) is limited to areas where *Hector* (the model) occurs: while the mimic of *Aristolochae* is as ubiquitous as its widespread model. This is one of the cases that strongly sustain the theory of mimicry. Even in its mode of flight, and in its habit of flitting daintily from leaf to leaf (though apparently not ovipositing) *Romulus* closely copies its model.

385. *Papilio helenus mooreanus* is a big black butterfly with three large white 'plates' on the hind-wing. It was obtained at Balangoda in the south of the Island, but was not seen elsewhere.

386. *Papilio Aristolochae ceylonicus* is common everywhere.

387. *Papilio agamemnon menides* (black with green spots) differs from the Malayan representative in having longer tails. He is plentiful, especially in Kandy.

388. *Papilio Doson* (black, with a broad diagonal line of blue 'plates') is more or less indistinguishable from the Malayan *Jason*. He is usually allowed to be the speediest of all butterflies, and one can hardly follow his flight with the eye. In April his behaviour was peculiar. He was

seen in considerable numbers travelling, usually in one direction (south-west), at express speed. I cannot remember having seen one settle at all during the dry season.

## PIERIDAE

389. APPIAS. *Appias Paulina* is very plentiful, and is often seen rising in whorls. There are two forms in Ceylon—*Lankpura* of the wet season, and *Galene* of the dry season. That is to say, the butterfly is seasonally dimorphic. In the wet season form especially, the colour of the reverse varies greatly from greenish-white to butter-yellow. At rest, the fore-wing is drooped in such a way that all the dark marks are hidden. The process is exactly the same as in the case of the English Grayling. *A. albina* is entirely white above, with the apex very lightly dusted.

390. *Byblia violae.* I am not sure in which family this butterfly should be placed. It is common in low scrub, and I have even noticed it up to 3000 feet. Its nearest relatives are two species of *Byblia* in Africa, and on this account it is one of the most suggestive and interesting butterflies in Ceylon. Besides a strong seasonal dimorphism, it varies very greatly even amongst specimens taken on the same day, which range from muddy-brown, through chestnut, to bright orange. The *palpi* are long and hairy, and are worth examining under the magnifying glass. It always seems to me particularly romantic when frail butterflies are found to be a link in the evidence of titanic earth-movements. *B. violae* is such a link: and *Aphnaeusa lohita lazularia* (para. 410), a little 'Blue,' with strong reddish stripes on the reverse, is another. In Ceylon these two have survived the break-up of a continent, since their separation from relatives across the Indian Ocean. The occurrence of the

same weak insect, often having identical habits, in islands and continents now widely separated, is not uncommon; but it always seems to possess a fresh wonder.

391. CATOPSILIA. The common one is the white and yellow *C. crocale flava* which is remarkable for the extraordinary migrations it undertakes in February and November. Flights which continued in the same direction for many days are mentioned by Forbes, who supposes that they arise from the necessity for finding new feeding grounds. The females are said to lay while migrating. The natives consider that these butterfly-streams are directed towards Adam's Peak, and it has been suggested that the Sinhalese name for a butterfly—*Samanaliya*—is derived from such beliefs. *Samanaliya* (see paragraph 273) is the word for a Buddhist Priest, and the yellow butterflies are supposed to be the spirits of departed hermits hurrying on a pilgrimage to the sacred mountain. A writer in *Spolia Zeylanica* (Vol. III, page 219) describes one of these migrations thus: "*Catopsilia crocale* and *Appias paulina* were most in evidence. But *Hebomoia glaucippe*, *Ixias ceylonica*, and the Papilios *erithonius*, *jason*, *crino* and *aristolochae* were associated with them. *Euplaea asela* was also on the move, but not in very large numbers. It was distinctly a flight of *Pieridae*, more particularly of the genus *Catopsilia*."

392. DELIAS. *D. eucharis* is very common, especially in the low country, though it is found also at all elevations up to 5000 feet. On the reverse of the hind-wing there is a marginal row of brick-red hearts which show through on the upper surface with a lovely rosy tint. The female is much darker than the male.

393. HEBOMOIA. *H. glaucippe ceylonica*, the large orange-tipped white, is common in the lowlands. The female is rare and was not seen.

394. Pareronia. The male is a pale green butterfly with black veins and margins. I did not see the female which is presumably a mimic, as in Borneo and Malaya. Even the male is not very common and is given to flying in the undergrowth.

395. Terias. *T. hercabe* is widely distributed and rather variable.

## DANAINAE

396. Danais. The common low-country forms are *D. aglea ceylonica : D. liminiace mutina : D. melissa musikanos : D. chrysippus* and *D. plexippus.* The highlands of Haputale and Horton Plain, however, possess *D. fumata* which is found nowhere else in the World. It is a very dark and handsome brown, with only two greenish splays on the fore-wing, and one on the hind-wing. In the limited areas in which it occurs it is quite plentiful.

397. Euplaea, *E. asela,* a plain brown butterfly with a margin of whitish spots, is quite the commonest butterfly in Ceylon. As far as I know, it is the only Euplaea. I did not identify any others.

## SATYRIDAE

398. Elymnias. A very curious capture, already noted in the text of this book (paragraph 232) was that of a female of *Elymnias hypermnestra undularis,* which was flying close to the spray of the great rollers that break on the rock of Dondra Lighthouse. This butterfly is not found in Southern India, but occurs again further north. The specimen was interesting also on account of the dissimilarity of the two hind-wings, the marginal dots being much larger and much less defined on one wing than on the other.

399. LETHE. Horton Plain is an open, grassy tableland, with an elevation of nearly 7000 feet. Some rare and interesting butterflies inhabit the plateau and the woods below—notably *Lethe daretis* which occurs nowhere else. One of the rarest flies I obtained in the Malay Peninsula was also a Letho-*Chandica Namoura*. The only butterfly I saw on Adam's Peak which looked in the least interesting was a Lethe—but I did not carry a net, for fear of hurting the feelings of the rather emotional pilgrims.

400. YIPTHIMA. *Y. ceylonica* is brown, shading off to white on the hind-wing, and with one large eye on the fore-wing.

## MORPHINAE

No single member of these great and shining butterflies of the deep forest was seen—*Amathusia*, *Discophora*, *Zeuxidia* and the rest.

## NYMPHALINAE

401. CETHOSIA. *C. nietneri* resembles the Burmese form, and is fairly common at 2000 feet.

402. CHARAXES. Near Dambulla I captured the dark brown *Charaxes fabius*, which has splays of yellow marks across both wings, and has four slender and elegant tails. The reverse is silvery grey, merging to bluish 'eyes' on the hind-wing. It is a good butterfly. Round about Maho *C. psaphon* is fairly common. The middle of the wing is whitish, bordered on the inside with chestnut, and on the outside with black.

403. CYNTHIA. The tawny yellow *Cynthia erota asela* is common. I frequently saw the lovely blue female at Kandy, but never captured her.

404. DOLESCHALLIA. I only saw and caught one specimen

—*D. bisaltide ceylonica*—which is close to the Andamanese type. It has no white spots on the apex of the forewing : and Seitz describes it as rare.

405. Hypolimnas. What I imagine to be *H. charybdis* (a large brown butterfly with a whitish-purple patch on each wing) is one of the commonest forest butterflies in Ceylon up to 4700 feet. The female *H. jacintha* is very different in appearance, being dark-brown with a cream-coloured border. She is comparatively rare, but I saw specimens at Haldummulla (3300 feet) and at Trincomalee (sea-level). At Kandy (2000 feet) I procured a very small species of Hypolimnas at the end of May. It resembled *bolina* as figured by Seitz (Plate 118. G.), but is at the same time very close to *misippus* from Borneo, figured in my 'Kinabalu' (Plate I. 18). *Misippus* has three female forms, which renders it as interesting in this matter of sexual dimorphism as *P. Memnon*. It is also seasonally dimorphic.

406. Junonia. Upon the grass-lands of Haldummulla flits that charming morsel of Heaven's blue sky—*Junonia orithyia*. *J. lemonias* is plentiful.

407. Mycalesis. The common ones are *M. Patnia*—a chocolate-brown with a large yellow eye : and *Mandate*—pale brown, with a broad white line on the reverse, which shows through faintly.

408. Parthenos. *P. cyaneus* is fairly common at Ratnapura, but I never saw it again anywhere else. There seems to be a greater disparity in the size of the sexes than I remember in other countries where Pathenos occurs. The female is very large and fine. She has a restless, jerky flight, and is hard to capture.

409. Vanessa. A familiar friend is *Vanessa cardui*, which is interesting on account of its extraordinary range.

Individuals from Haldumulla are identical with others from Burma, and with others again from England where we call them the 'Painted Lady.' Horton Plain has a Vanessa found nowhere else, namely *V. pyrameis nubicola.* It differs from *V. indica* in being much darker, and in having a rich crimson band across the fore-wing. I got it myself actually within a few yards of Ohiya Station : and *Lethe daretis* (paragraph 399) in the bamboo and rhododendron forests above. Something like a blue *V. canace* was once seen at Balangoda, but not captured.

## LYCAENIDAE

There are, of course, a great number of 'Blues' : but I propose to mention only a few :

410. APHNAEUSA. *A. lohita lazularia* is chiefly interesting because of the fact that its range extends to South Africa, and on that account, it has the same significance as that already noted concerning *Byblia violae* (paragraph 390). The upper surface of the fore-wing is dark-brown with some dull orange marks near the apex. The hind-wing is violet-blue, and has two hair-like tails with an orange patch at the base. The reverse is very distinctive, having strong bands of chestnut on a yellow ground.

411. CASTALIUS DECIDIA is black, with a white central area. The reverse is white with bold black markings. *C. ethion* is something like it, but has some blue as well.

412. CURETIS THETIS ARCUATA is rich orange-red, edged with black. The black is thickest at the apex. The reverse is plain pale bluish-white.

413. LAMPIDES CELENO TISSAMA is a glorious shining 'Blue,' with a twinkling flight. The reverse is brownish

grey, profusely crossed with white lines which have a tendency to show through on the upper surface.

414. Talicada nyeus. This extremely pretty little butterfly is common in the south of Ceylon from 500 feet to 3000 feet. It is dark brown with a big orange patch on the hind-wing. The reverse is mostly white, but is broadly edged on the fore-wing with black, and on the hind-wing with orange.

415. Zizera. *Z. otis* is one of the extremely small 'Blues.' It is dull blue, the reverse being grey with dark spots and speckles.

## MOTHS

416. At Haldummulla a great variety of moths may be taken at night with a lamp. Amongst those obtained was the Clear Wing (*Cephonodes picus*), and a form of Plume Moth. Kandy also is a good place for moths in May and June. Of these, the most astonishing are those which are too small to deal with in the ordinary way. Under the magnifying glass they reveal an extraordinary beauty and richness of colour and pattern, and a quaintness of shape that is amazing. It would be a delightful hobby, if one had the time and eyesight, to make enlarged sketches of these tiny moths. I am not aware that they have ever been classified. Silver, gold, and bronze have been lavished upon those almost invisible wings. One of the finest moths obtained was the handsome green Sphingid, *Rhyncolaba acteus*.

# INDEX

**Figures refer to paragraphs.**